I'M PREGNANT... NOW WHAT?

by
Sara R. Dormon, Ph.D.
and
Ruth Graham McIntyre

"A Resource of Choices for Unplanned Pregnancies"
www.forpregnancyhelp.com

ForPregnancyHelp.com, 4919 Township Line Road #220, Drexel Hill, PA 19026

Visit our Web site at http://www.forpregnancyhelp.com

First Printing: June 2002

ISBN: 0-9720822-0-4

Table Of Contents

In this chapter we explore the emotions and realities of facing an unplanned pregnancy. There is practical advice as well as first person stories. The practical advice will help you through the most important first steps of your pregnancy.

There will be times when it may seem as if no one cares, but that is not true. Here we give not only practical, pro-active guidance, but we remind you of what you may not be able to see or hear. You will also read stories of girls who have walked this path before you.

We will help you through the decision-making process to reach an informed, educated and workable plan. This is done by thoroughly exploring all of your options, with the help and input of your support network.

You have decided to release your child for adoption. The information here will help you to prepare for the day of release and beyond. You will know what to expect, what you will feel, not feel, want and not want.

A step-by-step plan to help you survive what will seem at times as though it can't be survived. We will give everyone involved tips on what you can do to make the unbearable, bearable.

Introduction

We have been where you are. Our book comes out of experience. This book has been written by many people who know what you are confronting.

If you are reading this page, you are full of questions for which you have few, if any, answers. People may be giving you answers but they don't really know your questions and don't seem to be listening to you. You are under a great amount of stress and pressure. You may be alone in your dilemma with no support from those who had made you promises. You feel rejected and betrayed. You are hurt and angry. We understand those feelings.

It is our desire to address your needs factually and encourage you. We will examine the issues involved from all sides and give you the best information available so you can make a decision with which you can live. We believe that an informed decision is the best decision.

We respect your right to make that decision and know the importance that it be yours to make. We also know that the decisions you make have long-term ramifications that affect not only you, and your baby, but others as well. We want you to hear from others who made decisions — how they arrived at their choice and how it affected them. These are real people in real-life situations. Their stories are told objectively so that you can draw your own conclusion.

The authors of this book believe that we are known of God before the foundation of the world. We are intricately formed by God in his image. While yet in the womb he knows our personality, temperament, body and mind. We are a living soul with a God quickened spirit.

We believe the Scriptures teach the sanctity of life. Life is a gift from God and is to be respected as holy and valuable. Life is life whether it is the result of rape, incest, marred by deformity or whether it threatens the life of the mother. It is life.

God gave us choice. He asks that we choose life, but we are sinners. The world is an imperfect place and we are confronted with difficult choices everyday. God knows our frame and remembers we are but dust and extends to us forgiveness of sin, mercy for healing and grace for living.

It is our commitment to life to encourage young women to carry their unborn children to life — there is no greater love. We know it is a costly decision emotionally, physically, and mentally. We do not condemn those who choose differently. It is our commitment to love and encourage those who have been deeply wounded by abortion.

We support the adoption option wholeheartedly but believe with as much passion that there must be long-term support for the birthmother. This is what this book is about — supporting and encouraging the birthmother, regardless of the choice she makes. We are not interested in politics, but in lives — lives of young women and men who have made mistakes and now face difficult decisions.

"Greater love has no one than this, that one lay down their life for another."

1

I'm Pregnant... Now What?

Ruth's Story — A Mother's Heart

Windsor was sleeping a lot. She would come home from school and take a long nap before dragging down to dinner.

She was keeping company with a young man who was pleasant but had few if any ambitions. I didn't prevent them from seeing each other, but hoped it would soon run its course.

I had wanted her to get involved in sports. She had enjoyed horseback riding when she was younger but had dropped her interest turning to an interest in boys. I gave her flight lessons and she seemed to enjoy those but soon this young man diverted her attention and I could see I was wasting my money. I encouraged her to try out for basketball, which she did, but she did not make the team. I remember well my keen disappointment and anger with God. I was trying to do my part, why couldn't he help me out?

She fell in with the crowd that had little ambition except to have a big truck and plenty of chewing tobacco. I had higher aspirations for Windsor. She accused me of being judgmental and not trusting her. Our relationship was volatile and frustrating.

She sat beside me on my bed. I saw fear in her big blue eyes as she confessed that she suspected she was pregnant. I tried to prepare myself for what may lie ahead as I embraced her, telling her it would be okay. Inwardly, I was far from confident but outwardly, my mind began to shift into overdrive as the adrenaline kicked in. I wanted to be calm for Windsor's sake — to reassure her. There didn't need to be two hysterical women!

I was not particularly anxious to have her suspicion confirmed and might have let it go on for several days, if not weeks. Denial is an amazing thing! I wasn't sure I was ready to deal with all that might come with finding out for sure. Confiding in a psychologist friend, she insisted that we go that very afternoon and have a pregnancy test.

After school as I drove Windsor to the doctor's office, my mind was racing ahead. How would we handle this? Could I protect her? And there was some concern for my own reputation: what would people say now? I was a single mom and I could hear the blame being cast in my direction. I was troubled by my thoughts. I felt guilty for being concerned about myself. What was I supposed to do now? I was not prepared for this — this happened to other families, not to mine.

Hours later in the doctor's office, when he confirmed her suspicion, I looked into her eyes brimming with tears and held her tightly as moans escaped from her inner depths. My mind raced as to how to protect her from what I knew was ahead.

Our lives would be changed forever.

I knew Windsor was wounded and did not need me to add salt to her wounds. I knew she was feeling guilty and shamed; I didn't need to add to it. I knew she was trying to fill the hole in her heart left by her father's neglect by "looking for love in all the wrong places". She didn't need more rejection from me.

We were both confused. I reached for my Bible, it opened to verses concerning peace. Peace! I was far from peaceful but it was exactly what I needed. As I read, "The Lord of peace himself gives you peace always by all means. The Lord be with you all." And "My presence shall go with thee..." I felt a peace that was not my own. I would return to those verses many times!

What do you do with the information that your sixteen-year-old daughter is pregnant? I couldn't shout it from the rooftops. I couldn't hide it under a rock for long. I couldn't ignore it and hope it would go away. It would do no good to run around in circles screaming! At some point, sooner rather than later, I had to confront the many issues involved. This ultimately would involve facing my own responsibility, guilt, shame and anger. In spite of my love, tears and prayers, efforts of discipline, yelling and screaming, I had watched my child make bad choices. Now she was bearing the consequences. Could I have done more? Watched more closely? Grounded her more often? Yes, no doubt I could have been her jailer. That would have only made the situation worse.

But, at first, we both needed to take a breath — get some time to think and pray and get counsel. Windsor's first decision was that she wanted to carry the baby to life — she did not want an abortion. I was thankful for that.

Windsor informed her boyfriend of her pregnancy. He did not love Windsor and did not want to marry her. He was young and scared — they both were. We met with him and his mother together with a licensed counselor trying to figure out what to do. The young man did meet with us several times and was honest about his feelings, though it cut Windsor to ribbons. The more he withdrew the more desperate she became trying to hold onto him. It wasn't long before he was gone.

We didn't know what to do but I wanted to find someone who could help us sort it all out. I needed to remember that I was the adult and my child was looking to me for help. I would be useless if I came unglued. My tears came later, much later.

I made hundreds of phone calls. I called the local juvenile court officer to find out the legal issues and what responsibility the young man had for this child. I asked if I could keep the young man away from Windsor. There were legal ways to do that. The young man would be entitled to visitation and would have a financial responsibility until the baby was eighteen years old. I inquired about statutory rape since Windsor was only sixteen — this did not apply in her case.

I called the local Crisis Pregnancy Center to find out what resources they offered. They told me that they had counselors available and met with Windsor a few times. They gave me names of "unwed mother homes" — I pursued each lead they gave me. The homes I called were far away or seemed to be rigid. Windsor had heard enough preaching and needed a balanced approach to the many decisions cushioned with a sense of humor. I didn't feel it had to be so grim. After all, this was life, not death. Everywhere I turned there seemed to be hidden — or not so hidden — agendas. Most agencies I called believed that young women should release the baby for adoption — few credibly told me that the choice was up to the young woman. Windsor did not want to be manipulated into a decision. The search was frustrating.

I called my pastor whose main advice seemed proscribed: that a child was coming and the young people involved were not capable of taking care of it. He suggested ground rules before he would advise me to support Windsor: she was to carry to term; quit seeing the young man and deal with the sin of the situation. The pastor knew they did not love each other and had already proven to be irresponsible.

He suggested several options: 1) the young couple could marry, 2) they could drop out of school and get a job before they marry in preparation for the arrival of the baby, 3) they could release the baby for adoption. Since Windsor had not retracted her faith and had a spiritual commitment, he told me that she needed to demonstrate spiritual leadership. If they decided to marry, he believed the marriage would not survive since ninety-five percent of couples who marry under these circumstances split up and those who remain in the marriage report they are unhappy and wish they had married someone else.

My pastor suggested we meet with Windsor and the young man, the young man's mother, Windsor's father and me, along with the youth pastor of the church. We met Sunday after church. Windsor was surprised to see her father — he had flown in from Texas, where he lived. She was angry and became verbally abusive. She would have no part of the meeting.

After coaxing, eventually she joined us. The pastor gave the young couple their options to move in together, to marry, or, for Windsor, to go to a home for unwed mothers. The young man responded first: he had no way of supporting her, admitted he did not love her and found her to be difficult to get along with and, finally, did not want to marry her. Windsor was deeply hurt by his betrayal. At the same time, she was shocked and angered that the minister suggested she move in with the young man without being married. Blatantly unwilling, she balked at the suggestion of going to go to a home for unwed mothers. She exploded. She felt trapped.

That meeting was a disaster! The young man walked away "scott free" while Windsor's whole life was turned upside down. The unfairness was keenly felt.

After the meeting, I felt beaten up. At odds with my own emotions, I was both angry with Windsor, wanting to shake her, and yet compassionate, longing to hold her and make everything all right. Why couldn't she see that I was trying to help, trying to do the best thing for all concerned? I was exhausted. The tension between needing to be wise and wanting to wash my hands of it all wore me out. I wanted to escape. And yet I knew there was no place that was far enough away that would take away the knots in my stomach, the anxiety in my mind, and the ache in my heart.

At home, Windsor's and my perspectives were very different and we clashed often. She was angry and I was the safest person to take it out on — and she did. She was verbally abusive; she blamed me for all that was wrong and wanted me to make it all okay. She pushed me away with one hand and held me tight with the other. It was a roller coaster of emotion and heartache.

My pastor told me that Windsor was in rebellion and I should pack her bag, put it on my doorstep and lock the door. I could not do that nor did I agree with his assessment of Windsor. I did not believe she was in rebellion. I tolerated more than I would have because I knew her anger came out of her woundedness. She was hurt — desperately.

She had been hurt by her father's neglect and favoritism. She was hurt by our divorce. She had many reasons to look for love in all the wrong places. I was not going to give her another one.

I loved — and do love — Windsor deeply. I cannot say I was ever ashamed of her. I grieved for her and with her. But there were times I could have strangled her!

Sara is a special lady in my life. She helped both Windsor and me at a desperate time in our lives. Through her personal experiences and practical applications underscored by her professional qualifications as a clinical psychologist, we knew we could trust her advice and counsel. In her sections throughout this book you can benefit from that same experience, advice and counsel.

Sara's Guidance

There are probably few things a daughter has to say, or parents have to hear, which cause as much immediate and overwhelming anguish. Most young women will try to deny that they are even pregnant for as long as possible. When you do finally confirm what you have suspected all along, your mother is usually the first one you want to tell, sometimes even before the baby's father. After the tears, anger, hurt, and just being plain scared, you must take action. You don't need to be told that you have choices. Abortion is one of them. We aren't going to say that we think that is a good idea, because from our first hand experience, we know that it isn't. We have counseled hundreds of young women who, after having the abortion, experienced an overwhelming sense of loss and grief. We are not saying this is necessarily the same experience for all women, but it truly does define the reality for many. But whether we believe abortion is right or wrong isn't the issue. In this country, at this time, it is legal and offers a choice for many with unplanned pregnancies.

(Check out the Fetal Development link in the "Links to Related Sites" section of www.forpregnancyhelp.com)

Even if you are thinking about your options, and decide to carry your child to term, your first two priorities are to find a doctor and a counselor. Taking care of yourself and your child should be the single most important thing on your list. This would include eating right, your body and take care of it because for the next months your body will be sustaining the life of another human being. Getting enough rest is also very important.

You need to find a good counselor, one that specializes in crisis pregnancies. This is a person with whom you need to feel comfortable and someone you trust. If you don't feel comfortable with a counselor you go to see, keep looking. This is the person who is going to be your confidant, advocate, and, for the next few months, your best friend and worst nightmare. You may want this person to be a woman or you may want him to be a man, such as a pastor. The decision is yours, so don't allow yourself to be told what to do or whom you should see. With your vulnerability, heightened emotions, feelings of guilt, you may simply comply with whomever is in authority so as to not make more waves. This is your boat and your journey, so they are your waves and you will have to learn to sail some uncharted waters.

Mary's Story...

I was scared, alone and thinking I was pregnant. A good friend, an older woman, took me to get a pregnancy test at Planned Parenthood on Valentines Day. I was pregnant for sure. As I thought about telling my mother, I could see my life pass before me. She would not be happy. I was right. She physically attacked me and I had to go home with my friend. I hid from my mother and the rest of the family for over a month.

Abortion was the only option my mother saw for me. I was so scared, and not being sure who the father

was, I felt she was right. After I returned home, my
mother, afraid of what people would think, sent me to a
maternity home in our state. I hated it and after a week,
I moved north to stay with my aunt. She too thought I
should have an abortion and went so far as to get me an
appointment for one.

Before this appointment, I was looking through
my biology book, and I looked up fetal development.
When I saw pictures of a baby as old as mine, I cried. It
was a person, a baby, and it was mine. I told everyone I
wouldn't have an abortion and again, my mother
became "very emotional". Everyone tried to reason with
me, which meant seeing things their way. I wasn't about
to change my mind. My aunt found a woman in another
state who was willing to take me in, counsel me and
home school me until the baby came. So off I went
again.

Another story, very different, but dealing with the same issues:

Windsor's Story...

The loss of my innocence and youth came with
just two words... "you're pregnant". Little did I know
that those words took away my life as I'd known it at
the young age of sixteen. The idea of it put me into an
emotional spin. This is my story...

For a couple of weeks, I'd not been feeling well,
struggling to get out of bed and trying to keep my

*breakfast in my stomach. My gut told me "you're
pregnant", but I delayed finding out for sure. Finally
with guilt and fear, I sat at the edge of my mother's bed
crying, probably pregnant and knowing my boyfriend
was ending things.*

*"I think I'm pregnant", I blurted out, sobbing in
shame.*

*My mother sighed. It represented all she wanted
to say but couldn't put into words. She put her arms
around me. For the first time in months, we both felt the
same — we didn't want to face the reality yet. In fact,
we spent the rest of the day trying to suspend any
definitive action, trying to escape finding out the truth.
Feeling the horrible possibility of pregnancy, we
preferred the bliss of ignorance.*

*After school the next day, my mother mentioned
a doctor's appointment she had scheduled for us that
afternoon. Devastated, I gave her dozens of reasons
why we didn't need to go. At first she understood and
even sympathized. The initial struggle to face the reality
of this situation was monumental for both us — we both
wanted to run away from it, pretend it had not
happened to me, or to our family. I gave my mother the
time of her life, but she finally managed to get me into
the car. During the entire drive to the doctor's office, I
was trying to convince myself I wasn't pregnant,
thinking that because my family was who they were,
God would protect them from this kind of situation. As*

the car. During the entire drive to the doctor's office, I was trying to convince myself I wasn't pregnant, thinking that because my family was who they were, God would protect them from this kind of situation. As we got nearer to the office, I began to curse myself and feel the blame for being in this predicament. I felt ashamed, confused, scared, lonely, and stupid. I pleaded with my mother several times to turn the car around. I wanted to go home where I felt safe from the reality I was about to face. My mother didn't have much to say. Something had changed in her. All of a sudden, I could feel her disappointment with me; our car became a box that had trapped me inside.

You will need to have a support network around you of people you love, trust and who are willing to walk beside you on this journey. As Mary's story illustrates, these may not be family members. These people will be some of your greatest assets on this journey. They will hold you when you need it, cry with you, keep you accountable, even be your sounding board. Sometimes they will just be present with you; sometimes that will be all you may want. If the birthfather is part of the picture, he needs to be included in this circle. No matter how the two of you feel about each other, you have created a life for which you are responsible. For that reason, working together on the important decisions and developing a good relationship for the time being needs to be an important goal for the two of you.

There are so many things you need to know, but right now you won't be able to hear them all. Take this book, keep it near your bed and journey exists, everybody's journey looks and feels different. So look forward with as much courage as you can muster, and hold on to the hands and hearts of friends.

Try and remember this: *no matter how out of control you might feel at times, you are in control of one thing, the life of this baby living inside you.* You and the baby's father are responsible for it's creation and its future. Don't let anyone tell you what you have to do. Accept advice and guidance from those you love and trust, but ultimately, the decisions are yours alone. They have to be decisions with which you can live.

Chapter 1 — To Do List

Birthparents

- Have your pregnancy confirmed by a doctor
- Tell your parents
- Tell the birthfather
- Get counseling
- Make an appointment with an OB/GYN
- Put your baby's needs first
- Have a meeting with the birth grandparents
- Rest and eat well
- Express your anger appropriately
- Maintain relationships with those who will be there for you

Support Network

- Be supportive and compassionate
- Encourage her
- Listen to her
- Affirm her as a woman
- Help the birthfather with his responsibility
- Get information from all sources
- Be aware of the emotional roller coaster and try not to get on it
- Remember your words have the power to heal and hurt

2

Who Cares?

Ruth's Story — A Mother's Heart

A mother, by definition, cares. Deeply. I wanted to take care of it all for Windsor; wanted to hide her under my motherly wing!

I had to let her take the full brunt of the consequences but I made the commitment to her — the day she was born — to always be there for her. A mother cannot forget her child. There is no divorce for parenting — no matter how much you might want one. Motherhood is for life.

I would be there to pick her up if she fell, but I had to let her fall and feel the pain of it. She thought I didn't care. It made my heart ache. A birth-grandmother has a double heartache. Your own heart hurts and while you are dealing with that, you watch your child's heart break. And on top of it all you attempt to manage wildly swinging emotions.

How could I show Windsor I cared? I listened and listened and listened some more and some more. I heard things I didn't want to hear. It was hurtful. Arguing was futile, but more often than not, I fell into that trap. I made a point not to break my daughter's confidences. She needed to trust me with not only her angry outbursts but her deepest thoughts and fears. Because I felt so guilty and like such a failure, I was tempted to try to make myself look better at my daughter's expense. It would have been easy to gain sympathy from others by playing the victim. I tried to steer away from that. I didn't put her down or make jokes about the situation. I tried not to constantly throw the situation back in her face and blame her for everything that went wrong. Yes, she had upset my life — big time. My life would never be the same — and that might not be all bad but, at times it seemed like it was. I thought she had shamed my whole family. How could I hold my head up in church? In public? I just did it.

Birth-grandmothers come to understand — either through faith or counseling — that everyone makes mistakes and mistakes don't have to be fatal. Some are just more visible than others. I saw then that folks at church have no cause to be self-righteous — the whole premise of the church is that we are all sinners! In being human there is no need for pride. The ladies at "the club" have made mistakes — they just happen to be good at wearing masks. I learned not to let others define me or my child and never to sacrifice my child for my reputation. I knew I would lose far more than I'd gain.

One way I felt I could show I cared was to take responsibility for my own issues. I couldn't put them off on Windsor. It was my anger. It was my doubt. It was my guilt and shame. And it was tempting to blame or put my issues off on someone. I had to deal with them myself. It wasn't a one shot deal — I had to confront my issues over and over again because they had a way of showing up when I least expected or wanted them. I tried to keep short accounts. These feelings were uncomfortable. I didn't like them — I still don't. Anger isn't nice. It isn't pretty. It is hard. But I knew that the longer I kept the emotions inside the heavier they would get.

One way I failed my daughter was that I rarely let Windsor see my emotions. I was so busy trying to take care of Windsor, to be all things for her, that I didn't let her see my own anguish and doubts very often. Women/mothers are by nature nurturers and caregivers, to the neglect of themselves. Eventually, I needed counseling. I needed to cry. I hollered when I had to. Another way to show I cared was to reveal my own struggle to take care of myself.

I wrote notes and letters to Windsor, gave her a permanent record of my love and concern. In the thick of it, words of love and concern can get lost in the shuffle but a note, card, letter can be read and reread. Someone has said that for every negative it takes seven positives. That is why Hallmark is in business.

Journaling is a great way of releasing emotion and thinking out a situation. Flannery O'Conner said, "I don't know so well what I think until I see what I say." If you have never journaled, get a notebook, date the page and begin to write. Write out the events and your thoughts and reactions to them. Write down quotes you come across that speak to your situation. The more you write the better you will become at it. I found that in the process of reflection and journaling, God met me in special ways, giving me insights and wisdom. Now is a good time to begin a journal, not as a record of the pain and hurt, but as an outlet for your thoughts. Journaling is a valuable tool, one that I have become committed to using for myself.

I will confess that I did not journal then, while Windsor was going through this. I regret it. At the time, it was all so painful that I did not want to put it down on paper. I felt by living it, then writing about it, I was going through it twice. I did not have the energy for it. That was my loss and my mistake.

As a mother, you know your child better than anyone and can trust your instincts. When the pastor told me Windsor was in rebellion and to treat her as if she were rebelling, I knew in my heart that that was not the case. I knew Windsor better than anyone else and I had to trust my own heart. I knew she was trying to fill the hole in her heart left by her father's neglect by "looking for love in all the wrong places".

I tried to be consistent, to set boundaries and stick to them. I wasn't always successful but I knew there was security in boundaries for Windsor and for me. They were set to make life at home as much a refuge for Windsor as for me. Good boundaries for us included things like with whom she could socialize. What time she needed to come in or call in and by making sure she kept appointments and kept up with schoolwork. These boundaries created conflict at times. Windsor felt that if she was old enough to have a baby and make a decision about its future then she was old enough to make other decisions on her own. She seemed to miss the point about the difference between "age" and "maturity". I needed support in sticking to the boundaries set — I depended on my spouse, friends, and family.

Admittedly, this is a complicated journey for anyone involved with a child in an unplanned pregnancy. Those who share the love ties in our lives are all affected. It is a journey uniquely experienced by the whole family. Grandparents, siblings, aunts and uncles are all gradually absorbed into the challenges and implications involved. Friends, too. This is too complex a journey to take alone. I found others to lean on, told them what I needed. I allowed those I trusted to comfort me. I let them take care of me — to an extent. It was hard for me to ask for help and be on the receiving end. I am much more used to playing the role of being in control and taking care of others. I found an able counselor who helped me sort out my feelings and helped me make decisions that were best for Windsor, her child, and me. I constantly reminded myself to ask "What is best for Windsor and her baby?"

It was a bumpy ride and often got messy. I felt like I was a pioneer hacking my way through a jungle of emotions and decisions. There were times I would have gladly given up or given in. But I knew that if I quit, it would be like writing across the sky, "I don't care." The implications of not caring and not taking care of myself would be far more disastrous. I would lose Windsor forever. My child's life and the life of her unborn child were eternal. My weariness felt eternal but I knew it was not. These relationships were far more important than what others might think, or the shame and guilt I felt, or my own desires.

By standing with Windsor, by caring, I knew I would not loose her. She was mine; entrusted to me by God. My ultimate concern for her was spiritual. I wanted her to know God's unconditional love, his forgiveness. I wanted her to believe that he could and would bring something good out of this, if she let him.

I had the responsibility and privilege to model his love for her. I didn't do it well but I did the best I could, with his help.

Sara's Guidance

There will be people who will care deeply about you and your unborn child — surround yourself with them! You will need some discernment though, for some, who seem to share in the excitement will soon be gone. They just don't know how to act or what to say; don't take it personally. You don't need to be told that your parents care and your mother cares very deeply, after all she too is a mother. Their caring may, however, look different than you had hoped for.

These people who have said they care in both word and deed, will do and say things that will irritate you, anger you, frustrate you and make you question just how much they do really care. What you need to understand is that caring about you and understanding what you are going through are mutually exclusive emotions. Though they love you, they have no idea what you are dealing with, and they never will, unless they have had the same experience. Don't hold that against them, they are doing the best they can. Remember they do love you and your unborn child.

Cherie's Story...

You may feel as though you are completely alone, just you and your baby. What you may not realize now is that your pregnancy will not affect you and your baby alone, but it will affect your parents, siblings and extended relatives to some extent, as well as your baby's father's relatives. Your friends will also be impacted by your news. Some may be all excited and can't wait to go shopping and do the fun things that come along with a baby, while others may feel upset by your pregnancy and grow distant.

It is very important to have a good counselor. To this day I am in touch with mine, some seven years after we met. Four different people gave Sara's name to my mother during the first week after I told my parents I was pregnant. That was not a coincidence, that was God. He put her in my life to help counsel me through my life's most difficult time, and through my most important decision. She not only dealt with me, she also spoke with my parents and met with my siblings, and helped them with their feelings about my pregnancy and all it encompassed. Again, my point is that this not only affects you, but it impacts your whole entire family in ways you may not see, ways you can't imagine that they may let you know about.

Once the confusion, excitement, turmoil and anger die down, there will be a few people left standing. These are the people that you will most likely have with you throughout this journey. You know they care, not because they say they do, but because they are there. Use them! Talk to them, listen to them, laugh and cry with them, just remember, you are not alone and people care in the best way they know how, imperfect as it may be at times.

These people will have other lives, jobs, school, friends and families. They are not pregnant. They are not facing the decisions you are. They are not consumed and overwhelmed by the situation. YOU ARE! Be patient with them, they are doing the best they can. This journey is uncharted territory for most people, including you, so don't expect too much or you will be continuously disappointed. You must talk and tell people what you want them to know. A good thing to remember is, as much as you would like it to be different, people don't read minds. If you want them to know what and how you are feeling, you must tell them.

You will be amazed at the people who do care. Before you tell anybody, you will have played out the worst-case scenario in your mind. Generally speaking, nothing is ever as bad as we expect it to be. There will be parents, boyfriends and friends whose reactions may be even worse than you expect, but they all eventually come around, once the dust settles. The longer we wait to tell people, the worse the scenario gets. Most people will handle it much better than you ever thought they would. They will be there for you no matter what. It is generally a good idea in these situations to give people the benefit of the doubt. Let them in and let them care for you. For those who over react or react badly, give them time and space. I have never seen a parent, sibling or friend walk away for good. Your friends will care and assure you that they will be there for you, babysitting, hanging out, whatever you need. They mean it as they say it, but it won't happen, not for very long anyway. Most teenagers do not want to spend Saturday night babysitting with their friends, no matter how cute the baby is. They will go on with their life, most of which will not include you. Your life has changed, theirs hasn't. As much as they want to show you they care, they really don't know how. Don't hold this against them again. Tell them how you feel and how they can be there for you, if they choose to. If they don't, accept that too, and hang on to those who can.

Chapter 2 — To Do List

Birthparents

- Listen to those you love and respect
- Confide in your parents, they love you and care
- Don't expect too much from too many
- Realize your friends mean well, but don't count on them
- You don't have to go through this alone
- Let others be there for you
- Include the birthfather as much as he wants to be included

Support Network

- Find a good counselor for yourself
- Write her notes and letters to encourage and affirm her
- Journal your thoughts and emotions
- Be realistic in setting good boundaries; be consistent
- Don't give up, be there for her
- Listen, hug, laugh

3

The Decision Process

Ruth's Story — A Mother's Heart

This was one of the hardest parts, approaching the time when Windsor needed to make a decision. As a mother, I knew what I thought was best and I wanted to make Windsor do it. It was hard to sit back and let her make the decision with which she could live. I knew the ramifications of the decisions she was confronting — I could see down the road. I knew what was ahead. I had years of wisdom and wanted to give her a crash course, but here is where I had to let go of trying to control her and the decision making process.

I found that I needed to walk beside Windsor, support her, and tell her over and over again that I loved her. The best way to support her was to help her gather all the information I could get my hands on so she could make the decision that was best for her baby. Ultimately, it would be her decision to make.

But a mother of a pregnant teen has questions to face as well. What was I willing to do or not do? Was I willing to have her continue living with me? Under what conditions? Was there room for her and the baby? If I didn't think she could live with me, where would she live? How much would it cost? Did I have a family member that would take her in? A friend? Was she going to be covered under our medical insurance as a dependent? Would the baby also be covered? What if there was a medical complication? And long term, if Windsor decided to parent the child, was I willing to help? Was there room in my home for both? Would she continue her education or get a job? How would I react when she resumed her social life? What would be the ground rules? Would she cooperate?

Being clear in my own mind, I decided what I could and could not do. Then I informed Windsor and the young man, who was deciding if he wanted to stay in the picture and be included in the future plans of Windsor and her child. Ultimately, my role greatly influenced Windsor's decision.

Making so many decisions with far-reaching consequences, I found that I needed someone to talk to — someone wise and grounded. My decisions impacted my relationship with my daughter and the baby. I chose to go to my pastor because he raised issues I hadn't thought of: the deeper questions of motivations, ego, and spiritual components. He probed to find out if I thought God was calling me to rear the baby with Windsor. He advised me to pray about what God would have me do. When I did pray about it I felt I could not take responsibility for Windsor's life and its consequences — she had to face those herself.

Common sense gave me the conviction that Windsor was not old enough or mature enough to parent a child. Parenting alone wouldn't make her grow up. I wanted her to be able to finish high school and enjoy being a teenager. For me to step in and raise the baby in my home was not best for the baby, Windsor or me. I had to let her go, knowing that God was at work in both our lives and the life of the child.

Once I made my decision I wrote it down. I wrote down my reasons, any advice from others that resonated in my thinking, any Bible verse that seemed to confirm it for me. I knew that there would be many days I would doubt myself, second guess myself. I knew I would waver. And once the events ran their course I did ask myself, "Did I do the right thing?" If I hadn't written it out, I would have forgotten why I had made the decisions I made. At a time like this, I found I needed a small circle of advisors that grounded me. I learned to turn a deaf ear to all the well-meaning folks who gave me their opinions.

The decision I made was not the one Windsor wanted me to make and the struggle began. I did not feel that Windsor was capable of raising a child. She did not have the maturity or stability that I knew it would take. This was not a way of avoiding my responsibility to Windsor but she accused me of many things, selfishness and abandonment being two. She was furious and tried her best to get me to change my mind.

Tough love is hard.

I also knew that Windsor could not live at home and continue with the same friends and activities. That was impossible on many levels. In addition, because I was unaware of families willing to take in young pregnant girls and care for them, eventually, I took Windsor to an out of state home for unwed mothers. This home was only too pleased to have Billy Graham's grandchild in their care. Windsor was strong willed and difficult. It was not a happy match.

She did have other options. If she wanted to keep the baby, support it and raise it, I would give her a legal emancipation. She could get a job and support herself and the baby. Harsh? No. We believed this was the best decision for our family. Also, I knew my limits — and Windsor's. It was a difficult decision and even more difficult to sustain.

Looking back, would I make the same decision? Yes. I have not once regretted it. Windsor was angry about it and feels I manipulated her to make the choice I wanted her to make. But even now she will also say that releasing her baby girl was the best decision she could make for her child.

Let me add a footnote here. Windsor did release her baby girl for adoption. It was one of the most painful things I ever had to endure. She seemed to stabilize for a few months and then began a self-destructive downward spiral that was agonizing to watch as she created sorrow upon sorrow for herself and others. Eight months later she was pregnant again. Girls who release their babies often do have another one — they have an empty womb, empty arms and an empty heart.

Her behavior had been so unstable and erratic that I began to think she might be mentally and emotionally unstable. With this second pregnancy I began to consider the possibility of abortion. It might not be the worst thing that could happen. I was emotionally exhausted. I did not think I could go

Abortion is something that goes against my values and beliefs. I believe it is wrong. I was desperate to find a solution to the terrible dilemma we were faced with AGAIN! There was no easy way out of this. There was no painless resolution.

These were fleeting thoughts, but an option that I did suggest to her at the time. A friend, who was a pastor and licensed counselor, while not in favor of abortion, did think that under the circumstances, it should be considered.

Windsor would not hear of it.

And so the decision process began again....

Sara's Guidance

This chapter can't be written without addressing the issue of abortion. In today's world, the most natural and normal thing for a sixteen-year-old girl to think after finding out she is pregnant, is that abortion is her only choice. Very often abortion is considered and as we know very often they follow through. In many cases, abortion is considered to eliminate not the baby, but the evidence of unacceptable behavior.

We have stated very clearly in the introduction to this book that we are very much in favor of carrying a child to term. It has been stated by the president of the National Abortion Rights Action League that, "No woman has an abortion she wants to have, only one she feels she needs to have." Abortion brings with it an immediate solution to the problem, but it can also bring feelings of regret, remorse, guilt and a sense of loss. If these feelings do happen, the young woman faces a very unusual situation. Abortion is legal and condoned by a large part of society. She has chosen to have the abortion and now she experiences a myriad of feelings. Where does she go with these feelings and who is going to understand? Why should she have these feelings about something she wanted to do and that is legal? I believe the answer to this is because women were made to give life, not take it away.

This story illustrates what I mean. A young girl I knew was accidentally killed by a man as she ran out from between two cars. He did not know her and was not held accountable for this horrible tragedy. Shortly after this happened, the man had a complete mental and emotional breakdown as a result of the accident. Now ask yourself: if a total stranger has a complete breakdown over accidentally killing a small child he doesn't know, what do you think a mother feels when she intentionally takes the life of her own child?

I think you might appreciate two brief, but critical, scientific facts regarding fetal development. These are facts that a lot of married women with children may not know. Three weeks from conception, a beating heart can be seen and heard inside you. Six weeks after that, measurable brain waves can be monitored. By any standard, this is a living person.

The following is a poem written by a young woman after she had had an abortion.

Never to see the sun
Play upon your face
Never to wipe a tear
That only a mother could erase

Never to hold you
Tenderly in my arms
And draw you near
And protect you from any harm

Never to hold your tiny hand
And help you on your own
Only emptiness and wondering
About a child that's never grown

Never to gaze lovingly in precious eyes
And tell you with all my heart "I Love You"
The only remnant I have
Is the silent pain
That will always remain.

The decision making process is a long, agonizing, painful and frustrating journey. Initially, you will do everything you can do to avoid this journey, from denying the pregnancy to believing "Mr. Wonderful" will marry you, and together you will all live happily ever after. Unfortunately, it's only you who is pregnant. More often than not "Mr. Wonderful" will not be there for you, at least not in the ways you need him to be.

Making an informed decision about either adoption or parenting involves solving problems well. As harsh as it seems, one of the best things to do is to sit down and answer the following questions:

- If I decide to parent my child where will I live?
- Can I live with my parents?
- Can I live on my own?
- Can I live with the birthfather?
- If I decide to parent, how will I support my child and myself?
- If I decide to parent, how will I pay our medical expenses?
- Am I covered by my parents' insurance?
- Do I need to get on Medical Assistance?

This is just the tip of the iceberg when it comes to the questions that need to be answered regarding whether you should decide on parenting or adoption. Many of the questions that need to be addressed have no right or wrong answer, since every situation is different and the people involved all have different agendas and needs.

You should make a list of pros and cons regarding both parenting and adoption. Remember even if the only reason you have for wanting to keep your child is because she is yours, that is reason enough. But is that what is best for your child? That has to be the bottom line focus of your decision.

Certain common threads continue to run through nearly all unplanned pregnancies. These threads are fairly constant regardless of the age of the birthmother, the involvement level of the birthfather, or the educational or socioeconomic level of those involved. One of the most common threads is that every young woman who ever has had the issue of adoption suggested to her will adamantly say, "I could never do that!" And it is usually said with great emotion. Those involved with the birthmother, especially, need to be prepared for the emotional roller coaster as they participate in the birthmother's wavering thoughts.

The mother of the birthmother must realize two very important things right at the beginning. First, she and her daughter are looking at this "unplanned pregnancy" from two TOTALLY different perspectives. The birthmother is a frightened, young woman who has no idea what to expect, while her mother is looking at this as a more mature woman who has given birth and raised a child. It is like two people holding the tail and trunk of an elephant. It is the same animal, just very different viewpoints. Secondly, the birth soon-to-be-grandmother must remember that she will use logic and reason in helping her daughter make her decision. Her daughter will often only have emotion and anger to fuel her decision-making process.

As a birth mother, if your decision is to release your child for adoption, your decision is both the most loving and the most excruciatingly painful decision a young woman can ever make. You feel the tug of war keenly. You are trying to make a win-win for all concerned, especially the child. Often young women with goals and direction, as well as support from their families, are more likely to see adoption as a positive thing that will enable them and their child to have a chance to grow up, mature, and achieve their potential. A second reason you might see adoption as a good decision is it would provide your child with a stable, two-parent family. This is especially true if the birthfather is not involved, for birthmothers are keenly aware of children needing a father. Yet most young women will only have one very strong reason for wanting to parent their child, "Because she is mine!" Again, this is the only reason you need to chose to parent. Even when you can make a list of 27 reasons why providing your child with a two parent, financially stable, loving home, that one fact, "Because she is mine!" is sufficient. Reason and logic take a back seat to emotion. Keep this as close to the front of your mind as possible: your decision is to do what is best for your child, not for you, your parents, the birthfather, or his parents. Your decision has to be made with the child's best interest at heart.

Parenting is a viable and real choice for many women facing an unplanned pregnancy. Just as all parents before you have found out there is no parenting manual that comes with the baby, parenting is something you just do. You will parent as you have been parented for the most part, unless you have made a conscious decision, as some do, to be the exact opposite of your parents. Parenting is a 24/7 job, with no pay, long hours and little gratitude, but it can be done. Keeping your child is not something you consider lightly, but you should get as much input as possible from as many people as you trust and respect. Talk to your parents and others whose parenting skills you admire. Ask them questions, let them give you the benefit of their experience and wisdom. To help you make the decision as to whether or not you should parent, seriously ask and answer the questions listed earlier in this chapter. You will most likely need someone to help you to answer these, your parents, friends, birthfather or his parents. You should price daycare if you will need it, diapers, formula, clothes, cribs, doctors, anything and everything you can think of that you will need to provide a home for your child and to parent. The birth grandparents, yours and his, should put into writing what they will and will not be able to do to help you. Your plan should be in writing and once you have finished it, go over it in detail with all those who have said they will be able to help you in any way. They need to know that you are serious and that you are going to be counting on them.

It has been our experience that a lot of young women facing an unexpected pregnancy want to keep their baby so as to have someone to love and who will in turn love them back, unconditionally. This is especially true with young women who do not have the involvement of the birthfather and who may not have a father present in the home. Those who are in the support system of this young woman must continually bring her back around to the "real" issues at hand. Very often her anger will be the fuel that keeps her going. She will be angry at everything and everyone, especially those who are there for her and supporting her. These are the people she knows she can trust to love her in spite of herself. It is at this time you must try very hard to overlook her behavior, which is merely a reaction to the situation and reaction to the situation and just love her. You do not need to excuse her behavior, you must just understand, endure it and love her.

To birthmothers, if there was only one thing you could hear to help you through this decision making process, it would be this: When you truly love someone, as you love your child growing inside you right now, you want God's best for that person, whether or not it includes you. As hard as it may seem, and at times it will seem impossible, realize that the person whose life is most affected by your decision is that of your unborn child. The best decision is planning the child's future. There is no right or wrong decision, only a decision that is best.

Additionally, with adoption come legal issues about which the birthmother and her parents must become aware. This is addressed in more detail in the chapter 14. For now, we need to say that if adoption is the decision of the birthmother, the birthfather must be involved and notified in order for it to take place. Often the birthfather becomes the persona non grata: the only emotion held for him is outright hostility. This is natural and normal. Regardless of whether the birth mother likes it or not, the birthfather has all of the same legal rights and privileges as she does.

As much as we would like to offer you one clear cut method for reaching your decision to parent or release for adoption, it doesn't exist. Everyone's journey is different. So is their destination.

Cherie's Story...

I was 17 when I got pregnant. My senior year of high school was supposed to be the best year of my life — and in a way it was because I brought my son into the world. But in another way this was the hardest time of my life. When a teenaged mother looks at adoption as an option, it is like you're saying, "Hey, if I've already made the most important/hardest decision of my life, then the rest must be cake." Not necessarily. But if it helps you too look at it in that perspective, then go for it. I was going to go to college either way — whether I kept this baby or not, so I had to make two plans one if I kept the baby, and one if I did not.

I was unable to get welfare because I was 17 at the time, so there was no medical assistance to pay my prenatal bills. The bills were split between my parents and my boyfriend who was a college student with a part-time job. I only had a part-time job, and no real money to speak of. I went on and applied to college and just chose schools that were close enough so that if I kept the baby and commuted, I would be within a reasonable distance.

With the help of my counselor, I also went on and planned how I would be able to raise the baby, traveling to daycare centers and getting prices. I went shopping and priced baby items — clothes and diapers, etc. I spoke with several other young mothers and tried to plan out how I would be able to go to school, work part-time, and still have time and energy to spend with my child.

My parents also made a list of rules that would apply for myself and the baby as far as how many hours a week they would baby sit, and when I could have company and how much they could help to support me, etc. I look at this list today, and I still feel that it might have been a little strict, though I can now appreciate that they did it with the best interest of the baby in mind. Now I can also appreciate how hard it must have been for them to sit down and actually have to write it. Of course they wanted me to keep the baby, but they were not in the position for my mom to quit her job to raise my kid. They were done raising their children and they felt very strongly that this was my child and my responsibility. They were the grandparents not the mom and dad.

I also tried to find any type of housing that would be available to my child and me. In my town, this kind of housing was basically non-existent.

Once I turned 18, I was finally eligible for medical assistance, and I could get my prenatal visits paid for and other "benefits". This so-called "welfare" was no joke either — just because it's free doesn't mean that it is easy to get, or that it comes without a hassle.

It would be wonderful to say there is a very straight path that everyone takes when faced with an unplanned pregnancy, but there is not. Every person is different, every situation is different and all the people involved are different. People express emotions differently. The best advice we can give you here is to know that whatever you think or feel is all right. Whatever emotions you are experiencing are normal. No matter how sure you are that you will not survive this experience, you will. You are a lot stronger than you think you are and as the saying goes, "What doesn't kill you, will make you stronger." This experience is what I think they had in mind when that saying was written.

What needs to be said here is no matter what your decision-adoption, abortion or parenting-it is a decision that only you can make and one that only you will have to live with for the rest of your life. This is a decision that is of great importance and one that has great value for all involved. It is a decision that can and most likely will alter the rest of your life, therefore it should be approached with your eyes and mind open not only to the present, but also to what the future will look like. Ask yourself the question," If I keep my child, where will I be and what will I be doing in 5 years?" Then ask the opposite, "What will I be doing in 5 years if I release my child for adoption?" It is also important to try and keep in mind that this small, helpless baby that is going to enter your life, only stays that way for a brief time. Babies turn into toddlers, teenagers and adults.

Chapter 3 — To Do List

Birthparents

- Realize your time is limited
- Get counseling from someone who specializes in this type of issue
- Explore all possibilities
- Understand there is no easy way out
- Know what your parents will and won't do for you
- Make sure you have a way to pay for the medical expenses
- Base your decision on what is best for the baby, not you or anybody else
- Include the birthfather in the process, if possible
- If you are comfortable praying, do it

Support Network

- Make a list of what you will and won't do for your child
- Be willing for the decision to be different than what you want or expect
- Be aware that you are not in control
- Give your child the benefits of your wisdom and experience
- Accept there is no right or wrong, only what is best for the baby

No Greater Love

Ruth's Story — A Mother's Heart

My daughter decided to release her baby. She changed her mind just about every hour — that's normal. Her emotions were all over the map so I needed to be steady and calm — at least on the outside! Windsor was on a roller coaster of emotion and vacillated to the very end — it nearly drove me around the bend. It is good to be prepared for this.

How does one prepare for such a bumpy ride? I knew I had to be grounded myself. I decided not to get on her roller coaster with her. It is easier said than done because Windsor pulled at my heartstrings and pushed all my buttons. I relied on my small circle of friends and my counselor to be my sounding boards. I have said it before and I will say it again, I wish I had journaled my thoughts more consistently. It would have helped me sort out my own emotions and kept me more aware of my own processing and insights.

I am a nurturer. Most women are — especially mothers. I found that this was the time for me to nurture full-throttle! My child needed me as never before but she was more difficult than ever before. Impossible might be a better word.

There were days I didn't want to face another decision, argument or emotion. I didn't want stamina, I wanted out. I needed to nurture myself during these difficult days. I used every resource at my disposal to nurture myself. I did things I enjoyed. I love to go antiquing, so I did. I enjoy the beach, so I went. I read books more for pleasure than ultimate value! I didn't lose sight of my goals. I was in school — trying to finish my college degree and that kept my mind on things totally unrelated to what was happening around me. I exercised regularly and began to jog several times a week. It helped to lower my stress level and I felt better. I found I had trouble sleeping and asked my doctor for a mild medication. There is nothing wrong in asking for help when you need it. I did and was glad to know I could get help.

I knew if I did not take care of myself I would spiral downwards emotionally and be of no use to anyone. This was a stressful time — what an understatement! For me, my depression was not so much a feeling of sadness but a sense of weariness; I felt like I was walking through wet concrete. I knew I needed medical help. It is not "more spiritual" not to go for help. I went to a doctor and asked to be evaluated for clinical depression. I found there are wonderful doctors and counselors who specialize in treating such an illness. Help is available — medicine can make a difference. I did not want it to get out of control. Others were depending on me.

Focusing on a creative project lifted my spirits and calmed my mind. I got busy making a quilt for the baby. When my first child was born I made a patchwork, gingham quilt. I used it for each of my three children when they came home from the hospital. I decided that I would make one for Windsor's baby. It served several purposes. It gave me a way of placing this child in our family. It was a symbolic way of saying to my daughter that this child belongs to us and this was a very important message for my daughter to hear from me. It was my special gift to this child that Windsor would be able to keep and use for any other children that might come later, thereby, connecting her children to each other. It was also a fun project that I enjoyed — keeping your hands busy when your emotions seem to be spinning out of control is very therapeutic.

And would you believe that through all of this I got married! I had already fallen in love with a wonderful man who also loved Windsor like a daughter. Since so much was going on in my life and we could not decide when it would be a good time to "have a wedding", we eloped! He was the partner I needed. Even today I am amazed that he decided to take us on at this particular time. Windsor's father was very ineffective during this time. Windsor and her dad had a volatile and distant relationship. My new husband became our gift; he was loving but firm. I wouldn't recommend you go out and get married during a time like this! My husband and I found that we needed to take good care of each other. We did not neglect our relationship; we needed each other more than ever. We talked a lot. We dreamed about the future. We planned outings and had fun. We held each other often.

Windsor began to focus on the process of releasing the baby. There were decisions that were hers alone to make. I didn't always agree, but I knew it was important to let her make them and then support her. These decisions ranged from who would be her Lamaze coach —did she even want one — to who would be in the labor and delivery room, even to the choice of adoptive parents for her child. Sometimes she asked for advice — I tried to keep it simple, recognizing that it was important for these decisions to be hers. Some decisions and reasoning seemed irrational to me. I knew that was okay. I had to let her make these decisions her way. I was not the one releasing my baby.

I found it to be a good exercise for me to take the time to imagine how it might be for me if I were in Windsor's place: the hurt and confusion of finding myself pregnant; the grief and betrayal of a young man who had declared his love only to leave when I needed him most; the anger at everyone and everybody; the saying goodbye to my teenage years while those around me were planning for the prom; the effort to make decisions while coping with guilt and shame. It was a difficult exercise and I cannot imagine the heartache of losing one of my children — especially a firstborn. To hold my child and know it is not mine to keep — it is only loaned to me for a few hours. I kept these things in my heart — I wish I had written them down in my journal and read them often so they could help me empathize with my child.

We began thinking of the process of releasing the baby and sought ways to make it significant. Windsor had never been baptized. My children had been dedicated to God in a ceremony when they were babies. I reasoned that they would decide for themselves as they matured when baptism would be most significant for them in their spiritual journey. One day in talking with Windsor by phone, she was discussing what sort of "ceremony" would be important as she released the baby. I mentioned the idea of a joint baptism with the baby. She liked the idea very much and contacted a Presbyterian pastor whom I had known for many years and who would be tender with all involved. So that is what we did.

Windsor was ambivalent about the idea that the adoptive mother would be present in the labor and delivery room; she asked my advice. I told her that I thought it would be special for the adopting mother to see the baby born but also important for the baby in later years to know that both mothers were there. She was adamant that she did not want the adoptive mother to touch the baby first. I see the significance of that choice now, for the consequences last. In the delivery room when the baby was born and put in the warming bed across the room, Windsor became agitated that the adoptive mother was standing in the way of Windsor's view of the baby. I asked Windsor if the adopting mother could hold the baby and Windsor agreed but has regretted the timing ever since.

These issues seemed inconsequential to me, but for Windsor, even the smallest thing became monumental. I tried to remember this wasn't about me; it was about the best way for Windsor to release her child. She had to decide what would give her comfort, not only now, but in years to come. My job was to be supportive. Young, unmarried, pregnant women are difficult. I took that into consideration and tried to keep my wits about me.

Sara's Guidance

Well, you have decided that the most loving and best thing you can do for your child is to release her/him for adoption. For your life situation you have taken the bravest, most courageous, most loving step a mother can take. That is the true mark of a mother, putting the welfare of her child before her own. There is no greater love. You will change your mind a hundred times before the actual birth takes place. And then, once you actually see and hold your baby you will assure everyone within earshot, "I CAN'T DO IT! I CAN'T GIVE HER UP!" That is what you mean and that is exactly how you feel. The mere thought of handing this beautiful, little person over to someone else who will watch it grow, kiss it goodnight, see its first step and hear its first word, produces an unbearable and unthinkable emotion so intense you believe you will die if you have to do it. We tell you now that adoption will mean immediate, intense grief, which will dissipate, but never stop. Keeping the baby will mean little pain at first, followed by a gradual ache which will develop into an intensity as painful as the emotional grief experienced by the birthmother in her adoption experience. What this means is, as the child grows and your life is altered drastically because of this child, you will experience the pain of a lost childhood, lost chances and lost opportunities. It is not at all uncommon for a birthmother who decides to parent to find a resentment toward the child building as she sees her former life slip away. Even in a society where being a single parent is now more common than a child having two active parents, single mothers have a special burden placed on them.

Either way there is pain, but you have chosen the immediate, intense pain that will diminish.

This is why your support network and counseling are crucial. You need to have them there to remind you that you made the best decision for the right reasons and what those reasons were. From the moment of birth on, you lose the ability to use the clear-sighted reason that you have developed over time. Hormones, emotion, and anger will fuel your decisions and words. You will be angry with everyone around you. Every fiber of your being will cry out: "NO! NO! NO! I won't go through with it!" But somewhere inside, in the deepest place of your heart, you know that this same love that says "NO!" will not allow you to change your decision. You will be able to release your child and you will ultimately act out of that deeper love for your child's ultimate welfare. That is the kind of selfless, unconditional love and wisdom that God only gives to mothers; for birthmothers, surely He gives an abundance of this love and an even greater abundance of mercy and grace.

Now, knowing this and having made your decision, at least for today, you need to begin to prepare for the day when you will release your child to the care of their adoptive parents. Believe in your heart this truth: you are now, and always will be, the mother of your child. Nothing can or will change that.

With this decision made, what you need to do now is talk to your doctors. Let them know you are planning on releasing your child for adoption and as your plans unfold, you will keep them informed. The reason for this is some hospitals may have rules as to how many people can be in the actual delivery room. They may require you to speak with the hospital social worker. All of these "rules" are meant for your benefit and protection. So, as intrusive as it may seem, try and be patient with the process. Your desires for your time in the hospital need a plan so you feel a sense of control. It is very important that you have your plan for the hospital stay ready well in advance. Do you want the baby to room in? Do you want the experience of nursing your child? Nursing, under these circumstances, offers no benefit to anyone involved and can really make the child's separation much harder than it needs to be. Additionally, who, if anyone, do you want to visit you in the hospital during this time? Do you want the adoptive parents there? Are they allowed to visit? Who leaves with the baby, you or them? Do you want a ceremony for the baby? All of these questions need to be addressed before the baby arrives. Most adoptive parents are willing to cooperate with the birthparents in any way possible. They realize that you're making the ultimate sacrifice for their substantial, life changing gain of becoming parents.

When you make your decision and your friends and family know, you will find that very few people will know what to say to you, especially after you have had the baby. They don't know whether to be happy or sad, and of course neither do you. There really isn't a Hallmark card designed for women releasing their babies for adoption. That should change and will. If any single group of women on the planet deserve balloons, flowers, champagne and cards then birthmothers win.

Mary's Story...

"I was 14, in the ninth grade, not sure who the father of my baby was and working for the first time in my life. It was only at McDonalds and I was only making $5.25, before taxes, but I was determined to keep my baby. I thought I could do it on my own, even though I *had no place to live and no support from anyone in my family. I was too young to even sign a contract for an apartment, but no one was going to talk me out of keeping my child. This child would love me unconditionally which I felt I had never experienced.*

My counselor encouraged me to at least think about the possibility of providing my child with a two parent, stable, financially secure home, but my pride and my love for this child was getting in the way. I looked at profiles of couples as much to humor my mother and my counselor as to actually find a home for my child. To really look seriously would be admitting that I couldn't do it and I wasn't ready for that yet. After a lot of talking, more crying, and realizing that my "fantasy" was just that, I looked at several couples. I liked two of them and wanted to meet them. I thought for sure I would like one more that the other, but I loved them both. Now I was faced with another hard decision, to whom should I release my baby. After a couple of weeks, I finally decided on one of the couples and they had a party for me. I met all of their siblings, their parents, all of my baby's cousins and everyone that was special to them. I knew deep down inside I had made the right decision for my child, but it still hurt like hell."

One of the purposes of this book is to help put a new, less threatening face on adoption. We want to make it as viable an option for young women facing an unplanned pregnancy as abortion or parenting.

There are fewer than 50,000 babies released for adoption in this country every year. There are also more than 500,000 couples trying to adopt a child at any given time. You do the math and you will see why so many couples travel out of our country to adopt. There are 1.4 million abortions every year, so if even 10% of those women decided on carrying their babies to term and releasing them for adoption, nearly half of those trying to adopt would be successful. The decision to release an unplanned baby for adoption to a couple who would love to become parents is a mature demonstration of great love.

Chapter 4 — To Do List

Birthparents

- Keep writing to your child
- Make a list of the things you want for your adoptive family
- Have a list of questions for the family
- Review profiles of potential families
- Decide who would be present at the birth
- Decide how long you want to spend with the baby after it's born
- Try to prepare yourself for the release of the child
- Discuss a ceremony for releasing the child
- Write down why you are giving the baby up for adoption and read it all the time

Support Network

- Affirm and support the decision for adoption
- Journal
- Help the birthmother prepare for delivery
- Rely on counselor for help
- Nurture your child and yourself
- Do things that you like doing
- Listen
- Flowers and gifts are appropriate
- Begin to focus on the future
- Have a special "shower" for the birthmother after releasing the baby

5

Taking Care Of Yourself

Ruth's Story — A Mother's Heart

In the previous chapter, I talked about practical ways I tried to take care of myself physically, emotionally, and mentally. How did I take care of myself spiritually? It was a vital key to my survival.

For many years I have made it a habit to read the devotional "Daily Light" everyday and write down the verses that spoke to my heart on any particular day. I didn't stop when Windsor got pregnant. I needed it more than ever. I kept a prayer diary. I recorded the things I was praying about for Windsor and her baby as well as the others involved and my other family members. It was my aim to do this each day. Mostly it was sporadic. God understood this. But these familiar practices were an anchor for me in very turbulent waters. It was good for me to keep routines when so much seemed to be out of control; they gave me a measure of stability.

For me, reading the Scriptures brought great comfort. I loved reading the Psalms. King David wasn't afraid to speak his mind to God, but yet he always came to a place where he could worship God — he gained perspective and equilibrium. The books of Job and Lamentations gave expression to the depths I was experiencing.

One of the main issues I had to deal with was forgiveness: forgiveness for my daughter, forgiveness for those around us who let us down, forgiveness of myself and a thousand little things along the way. I learned forgiveness is a choice; a decision. Then the decision must be worked out in the every day.

I'm not a "pie-in-the-sky" type of person. I'm not a person for pat answers. I am a person who likes to deal in reality. Often forgiveness is presented as a quick solution — "just forgive!" It isn't. It is a decision that brings God to the wound in your soul and begins the healing process. And it is a process. It takes time. Frequently, it is two steps forward and three steps back but, discouragement, while common, is less powerful than the daily decision to forgive.

It is like working a weak muscle. By realizing that something is terribly wrong, you've begun the work of getting healthy. You're given exercises to stretch that muscle. At first it feels so unnatural; the muscle gets sore and stiff but you remain committed and exercise daily. Soon you notice more flexibility and strength. You are able to move freely and find it hard to imagine a time when you didn't have the full use of that muscle.

Perhaps, as you read this, you are not particularly spiritual — now is as good a time as any to start to develop this side of you. Or perhaps you are very angry with God and would rather not deal with him. Nothing you can do or say is new for God, he has seen and heard everything. He is bigger than your anger and you are going to need him to help you make sense of all of this. Faith will transform your pain and loss. It doesn't make it "easier", it doesn't take it away, but you have someone who will never leave you or forsake you. And he will strengthen you, guide you, and even bring good out of it.

Your daughter's pregnancy didn't take God by surprise. He sees the end from the beginning. It helps to be in touch with the one who sees ahead because you will be in the dark most of the time!

My life had been altered by Windsor's bad choice. I did not expect it or want it, but here it was dumped in my lap. Not only did people look askance at Windsor but also at me. After all I was her mother. I was mad — angry is a better word! Angry at people, angry with Windsor, angry with the young man, angry with myself and anyone who happened to cross my path. I was angry even with God. It wasn't always rational. It just was. I wanted to lash out and frequently did, causing more damage. I was angry with myself. It threatened to spiral out of control. It was affecting my life, spiritually, emotionally and physically. I had to do something.

I just wanted it to all go away. But it wouldn't. I was tired of working so hard to just "maintain". But I had to unload the anger. It began with forgiveness. I made the choice to forgive. I told God about my decision and asked for his help in carrying that decision out. It started slowly. The first day I had to remind myself of that decision one hundred times. I had flashes of anger and words slipped out that I hadn't wanted or intended to say.

Forgiveness is like the blow up clown that is weighted in the bottom. You punch it and it falls down only to right itself. Our emotions hit us hard — often when we least expect it and knock us over. But the choice to forgive will right us again.

When I found out Windsor was pregnant, I was more concerned for her — anger came later. I wasn't angry with the young man; I felt pity for him. He was in way over his head and unable to cope. Anger needs to find someone to blame. I blamed Windsor's father. He had not been there for her as she grew up; he had rejected her early on as he became involved in adulterous affairs. He had left a huge void that she desperately wanted to fill. (The impact of a father's influence on young girls cannot be overstated. A father is key to a girl's self-image and self-confidence.) Then when the church let us down I was angry with it — why couldn't they help us? I was angry with God. He had let me down — couldn't he have intervened? I had enough anger to go around!

I knew that the only one my anger hurt was me. I had heard that often enough and now I knew it to be true. So what was I going to do about it? I made the decision to forgive. No, they (Windsor, the young man, her father, church) didn't deserve my forgiveness. They had wronged me. I couldn't wipe the slate clean. I couldn't pretend it wasn't there, even if I did put on a pretty face and cover it with a smile. I knew forgiveness was the only way out for me.

Forgiveness is not a matter of "time heals" or putting distance between you and the offender. It doesn't mean being blind or stupid or tolerant of bad behavior. It isn't forgetting. It isn't denying or excusing or avoiding conflict. It isn't excusing the consequences. Forgiveness looks the hurt straight in the eye, calls it for what it is, and says, "I relinquish the right to make you pay. I give you the opportunity to make a new beginning." It is costly. It isn't natural. Revenge is natural.

Forgiveness is a "God thing". And it is amazing to see what God does once we let him into the situation through the gate of forgiveness.

So I made the choice to forgive, I said the words. My heart had been deeply wounded and the process wasn't always smooth or pretty. Like the unused muscle, I was stiff and sore. Indeed, I did feel beaten up. But in a strange way, the stiffness, unnaturalness of forgiveness served to remind me all over again of my need. The more I put it into practice the greater my capacity for forgiveness became.

What if my daughter never asked for forgiveness? What if she continued to hurt me with her choices? Even that couldn't stop me from making the decision to forgive, and I appropriated that decision in my every day activities. Forgiveness could only come from me. I saw it as a choice and responsibility. I didn't wait for someone to ask for my forgiveness — I gave it. Once I had made that choice, I had done my part. I stood ready whenever Windsor might ask, if she ever would.

Each time I was reminded of what Windsor had done, I appropriated my choice to forgive. Someone has said it is like a bank deposit. By choosing to forgive you have made a large deposit in an account. Each time you need to draw on it, it is there ready. We have to draw on it for it to be of use.

Forgiveness is to be given freely — no strings attached. Forgiveness is unconditional; reconciliation is conditional. Reconciliation needs to see repentance and changed behavior — words alone don't cut it.

Perhaps my hardest moments were when I needed to ask for forgiveness for my offenses. It was tough. It was and is humbling. My whole nature rises to my defense and becomes indignant: "I am not perfect. Obviously, I didn't do it all right." I needed to go to Windsor (the young man, my spouse, my church and especially, God) and ask forgiveness for my resentments, harshness, and anger whatever my offense might have been.

For Windsor and me, it has taken years to uncover all the areas that have needed forgiveness. We try to address them as they come up, as God brings them to mind. It isn't easy. Recently we were up late talking. Windsor was telling me that she didn't think I had forgiven her. She was feeling that I was keeping her out emotionally. I was. I told her that she had truly broken my heart when she walked out of my house, rejecting all that I had provided, all my hopes for her and rejecting my love. I told her I had never gotten over it and I would never let her hurt me like that again. I was protecting my heart. She told me that I had never told her that before and she asked my forgiveness. We both cried. Healing continues to occur.

Sara's Guidance

The physical and emotional care you give yourself and your child is very important. This is, to say the least, a very stressful time, and stress affects us at levels we don't even realize. Because your baby will feel the same emotions you feel, as best you are able, try to minimize the stress. When babies hear what is going on around them, even though they can't understand the words, they can feel the tension and volume. If you are smoking, drinking, doing drugs or having unprotected sex, STOP, STOP, STOP, and STOP! Now it is time to think of your child's welfare. Draw on the power of becoming a mother. Live with a committed love for your unborn baby.

A good way to reduce the stress in your life is to exercise. You will need to get your doctors permission and remember you are not training for the Olympics, you are taking care of yourself and your baby. Talking to those whom you consider part of your support network is also good for stress relief. You often don't want answers or guidance, you just need someone to talk to. Do things for yourself that you enjoy, read, walk, listen to music, shop, whatever helps you relax. Your baby will benefit and so will you.

One concern every birthmother has is that you don't want your child to think you released them for adoption because you were selfish, didn't love them, or just didn't want them. Writing to your child in a journal can be a very useful gift for you and your child. You need to get yourself a blank paged book and every day, write to your child. If you think it is a girl, choose a name, the name you would give her, and start

every page with "Dear Sara" or, if it is a boy, "Dear David". Tell the child
exactly how you feel. Write about yourself, the father, the grandparents,
aunts and uncles. Explain how and why you made the decision to release
them for adoption; tell about how you selected the adoptive parents.
While telling them, you will also be reassuring yourself. This journal is
something you will give to the adoptive parents; so if you want to have it
for yourself, be sure to make a copy. Of course, this could also be done
on the computer. It is something your child will read when they are old
enough to ask questions and understand. These are your words, your
feelings, and your emotions. You are not leaving any significant
questions unanswered and, most importantly, you are not relying on the
adoptive parents to speak for you.

Cherie's Story...

Mentally — I felt so emotionally drained and up
and down that I did not know how I was going to make
it through. As if life is not difficult enough, and
pregnancy is not enough, add unplanned pregnancy and
a decision to make for you and your child, then
contemplate the rest of your life — either as a parent to
this child, or as a birthmother without your child. It's
important that you take care of yourself — get prenatal
care take your vitamins. It's amazing what I could do for
my child that I couldn't do for myself. I remember eating
right, walking daily — all this just for my baby. I loved
him so much, and I wanted the best for him that my
needs became secondary.

Spiritually — I felt very guilty for sinning and for doing what I had done. It's not like I was sleeping around and didn't know who the father was. I had been in a relationship for some time, but we were out of God's boundaries of blessings — yet not out of God's thoughts and love. A sin is a sin; my boyfriend's and my hidden sin was now public. I know God has forgiven me and I have learned to forgive myself. This was not the end of the world though it seemed that way at times. God promised He will never leave us or forsake us. Jesus died on the cross so that sins like these would be forgiven. His forgiveness doesn't give us the right to continue living contrary to His boundaries.

I felt like I was letting my parents down big time, and I wanted their forgiveness. My pregnancy also made me very appreciative of my parents and all they had done for me. Faced with the possibility of raising this child alone, I was so grateful that they had not thrown me out or forced me to get an abortion. It was my choice, and I thank them for giving me the option of having a choice, and not saying "this is what you are gonna do — final answer." Once I saw how expensive and time consuming, and all it means to have a child, I was so grateful that they were there for me and supportive. I can remember going to church every time a child was dedicated and just sitting there crying. I was wondering is this going to be me here with my child next year? Will I be up there all alone — a single mom? Or

will this dedication be going on somewhere else, and I
won't even have a clue that it is happening in some far
away town where my child will live with his new family.
It was very hard to go to church altogether, because I
was so full of guilt and all the emotion that comes with
pregnancy anyway — let alone the awesome decision
that lay before me to be made in the next few months.

It is also a good idea to make some sort of tangible gift, i.e. a
blanket, a collage of pictures, anything that will someday have a special
meaning to your child. Something that can reinforce the incredible love
that allowed you to provide for them something you couldn't.

Mentally, you also need to begin to prepare for the actual birth.
You need to take birthing classes, have a birth coach, and decide who
you do and do not want to be present at the birth. Decide if you want
the birth video taped and if yes, by whom? Remember, you are in
charge, but you need to be very clear about what you do and don't
want. The one person you will most likely want with you is your mother.
There is probably not another time in the life of a young woman where
she will want and need her mother more than when she is giving birth.
But remember, you and she are not looking through the same set of
eyes or feeling from the same heart.

As much as you would like to ignore the spiritual side of this
dilemma, you can't and shouldn't. Regardless of your religion or lack of
it, the life inside of you is growing, was created by God. As hard as it is
to believe, God loves this child more than any human ever could. God's
love is eternal. You may feel anger toward God for "letting me get
pregnant". But the truth is, you and the birthfather "made you get

pregnant." You may feel shame for being an unwed mother and that is very natural, but where you are and what you are facing is the result of a bad choice. You may not believe it, but someday you will, that there are many worse things that could happen to you.

God loves you deeply and passionately. He will forgive you and if you ask him, he will personally help you through this experience and all experiences yet to come.

Chapter 5 — To Do List

Birthparents

- Keep writing to the baby
- Talk
- Make things to send with the baby
- Read things that feed your soul
- Keep on with your life goals: if you don't have any, make some.
- Take care of yourself and your baby physically

Support Network

- Listen
- Make things to send with the baby
- Enjoy the relationships in your life
- Encourage birthmother to keep her goals

6

No One Can Love My Baby
As Much As I Do

Ruth's Story — A Mother's Heart

My daughter spent nine months thinking of very little else but the baby within her. This was literally heart of her heart. She loved this child more than anything. It was the one person who had walked each step of the way with her. This baby had filled a hole in her heart that nothing else could do. It had been her focus. I spent nine months thinking about Windsor *and* the baby — my focus had been both of them. My heart was divided.

I could see down the road, the grief of the separation and good-bye. I saw the agony of self-doubt, the heartache of loss. I could not spare her from the inevitable pain — I wanted to but my role was to just "be there". Because Windsor had decided to release her baby for adoption I did not think I could afford to give my heart away. This was an area of great consternation to Windsor. She accused me of not loving her child. I did and do love this child. That little girl is my first grandchild.

But she was loaned to us for only a few hours. I had to hold her and know she was not mine to keep. I longed to see her grow up, to hear her laugh and call me "Grandma". There is a unique ache in the heart that does not go away... a lump in the throat that arises at odd moments. There are times I think I have "gotten over it" and then the pain comes again...I am not sure one ever gets over it.

In some ways I think a parent's pain is worse. We know in anticipation of what is ahead... we have walked the path longer... we have our own grief to bear but then we watch our child grieve... Life doesn't prepare us for this. I know the peculiar heartache of watching my child's heart break. Not once, but repeatedly. I had to let God work his work in her life — no longer able to shield her from the permanence of loss and the depth of grief.

As the birth-grandmother, you and I play a unique role. Our daughters will give away the one thing they cherish most in all of their young lives. "No greater love..." They have laid down their life in sacrificing their health and their reputation by carrying the baby to term. They have walked through the valley of the shadow of death by giving birth. They have fallen in love and not withheld their love for the one they cannot keep. And having fallen desperately in love, they take the unimaginable step of giving that most precious of loves to the waiting arms of another woman.

These young birthmothers do not think anyone can ever love that baby as much as they do. They are correct; the adoptive mother demonstrate such sacrifice and love. They never voluntarily give up their baby.

I have never sacrificed as much as my daughter. I admire her courage. Because I kept many of my emotions to myself, she did not think I cared. Looking back I should have let Windsor see more of my emotion. There were times I felt that if I began, I would come unraveled and I felt Windsor needed me to be strong. She didn't, she needed me to share and feel her feelings.

Sara's Guidance

You won't get any arguments on this statement, "No one can love my baby as much as I do". While no one will ever love your child in the same way you do, they can and will love them as much, just in a different way. There is a unique relationship a mother has with her child from the moment she finds out she is pregnant to the moment of birth. Babies become a part of you in every way, physically, emotionally, mentally and spiritually. You will give your child a name even though you may never say it out loud. You will feel strongly if it is one sex over the other. You are this child's mother in every way, except the one that matters the most to you right now: taking your bundle of joy home from the hospital and living happily ever after.

Your decision to release your child for adoption, keep telling yourself, was made in the best interest of this child, a decision made because there is no greater love than to give your child the best possible life, even though it doesn't include you.

Cherie's Story...

When Nancy, the adoptive mother, came to the hospital after my son was born, she came in the room and asked to hold him. I just about threw up when she held him and put her pinky finger in his mouth. How dare she touch my baby? It made me so mad to see her holding him...I just wanted her to go away. This was my time, our time with my family and our baby. It took all

of me to let her in there, but I knew that she needed to
see him, and bond with him right then, as he was only a
few hours old. I look back now and think — "Duh, this is
the person that you are trusting to be this child's mother
for the rest of his life, and you can't let her hold him?" I
thought she was going to do a lot more than that. As
hard as it is, I think girls need to see adoptive parents
with the baby. After all, they are that child's parents. I
know of two other girls who did not let the mother hold
the baby, or made a big stink over it, and I felt like they
needed to give a little more of themselves to realize that
the adoptive parents need to be with the baby too.

      Nevertheless, I feel very strongly that the birth
mother needs to spend time with her child. There is a
fine line that exists as far as how much time is too
much, as far as getting overly attached and making the
letting go more difficult than it already is. There is no set
time as far as how much you should spend. For me, it
was very important that I got to spend time with him
and my boyfriend alone, just the three of us. Our little
family — even if it was all a fairy tale, it was nice to be
together. It was also important to me that my parents
spent time with the baby, and my siblings came to be
with him as well.

      My son was here for several days before he
could legally leave the state. I felt I did not want to
bring him home with me because it certainly would be
harder to let him go, and I would have memories of him

in the house, and in my room. We had a "ceremony" the night he left. My family, my boyfriend's family, and the adoptive parents were present. A minister prayed, and we all shared and passed him around. It was the hardest thing I have ever done, walking out that night without him. But God got me through it, and I knew that this was the best decision for my son. So what, my heart was ripped out and I thought I would die...I did heal, and I am thankful he is alive and thriving in his home with his family.

I think naming your baby is important although you must understand that your baby that you gave birth to is now their child, and they can name the baby whatever they please. I chose a few names and told the adoptive parents that I would be honored if they would even consider naming him one of the names we chose — either first or middle name. I understood that he was their son now, though, and they could name him whatever they chose. It was also hard in the months and first year or so after he was born to hear him called by the name given to him by them, Jesse. In my mind, he was Isaiah — and in all the letters and conversations his name was Jesse. It took me a little over a year or so to begin to accept that they named him, and that his name was Jesse. When he answers, it's because someone called him Jesse. He does not know the name I gave him at birth. I think that was a big step being able to accept that, and realize that Jesse was his name now, and when he is grown, he will answer to his name, not the one I gave him. I figured I better get over it and accept the fact that there was nothing I could do to change it. I think it also helped me to distance myself, so to speak, or help me accept a little more that he is THEIR son. He will always be my child, but they are his parents and he is their son. Our son.

Love is a very abstract term, meaning different things to different people. Love doesn't look or feel the same to everyone. Your love for your child is the most selfless love there can be. Your love is sacrificial, and it transcends what most people will never understand. You have become, at a great cost, a member of a very special group of women, the birthmother. From this day forward, until your time here is over, you will always be this child's mother, you have just given someone else the gift and privilege of raising him/her.

When we look back at the title of this chapter, "No One Can Love My Baby as Much as I Do" having read about these experiences, it has a whole new meaning. It is true, no one will ever love your child as much as you do and you have proven that by this completely selfless act and by enduring the pain and heartache that has no words. This is what mother love looks and feels like.

Chapter 6 — To Do List

Birthparents

- Keep writing to your baby
- Accept that others can and will love your baby
- Allow others to love you and your baby
- Give the baby a name and get your own birth certificate

Support Network

- Listen to the birthmother
- Have "outside" friends and counselors listen to you
- Don't be afraid to show her your emotions
- Allow the new child room in your heart
- Birth grandmothers: Verbalize to your daughter your admiration and your emotions
- Birth grandfathers: Be there for your daughter — share what you feel

7

The Man's Viewpoint

Ruth's Story — A Mother's Heart

I cannot say I was angry with the young man. I just wanted him out of Windsor's life. He was not someone that was committed to her or the little life she carried. I certainly did not see any future with him.

Both he and his mother met with us and a counselor to talk over his plans. It was an awkward meeting to say the least. I came away angry at his mother's naiveté as she made excuses for him and gave a grand picture of him wanting to go on to the university — he was not college material by any stretch of the imagination. His ambitions were low and our expectations, lower. He was very up front about the fact that he did not love Windsor and did not want to marry her.

But the young man did seem to feel some responsibility — I will give him credit for that — he just was not willing to carry it too far. He was young and scared.

As noted earlier, he met with our pastor and us as the pastor spelled out options and conditions. He told Windsor she was angry with him all the time and he didn't like to be around her. He was not in love with her and did not want to live with her. It was so hard for her to hear. Tears coursed down her cheeks as his words broke her heart. He had made so many promises. He had told her he loved her and she believed him — she desperately wanted to believe him. Now it was all collapsing around her and she was going to have to bear the consequences for the actions of both of them, *alone*. He humiliated her in front of the pastor, her family and his mother. Truly, she felt alone and betrayed.

My heart ached to watch this play out — even though I had predicted it more than once as a warning to her. "I told you so" was not appropriate — ever. She was very aware that she had been warned and ignored it. Regrets are so very hard to bear. She knew she was at fault. Her anger boiled over and she took it out on me.

But my heart broke for her. Her childhood was over. Her dreams, dashed. And he just walked away. She wanted revenge; she wanted him to pay in some way. I couldn't blame her but I knew that there was no adequate way for her to feel satisfied. There would be no justice. I just wanted us to survive!

He did walk away and we never heard from him. Windsor kept in touch with his mother from time to time. When the baby was born, Windsor took pictures by to show her. His mother called the house one day, and I answered the phone. She said she cared about Windsor. I lost it! She who had not given so much as a quarter for a Coke for Windsor during this whole ordeal! I told her never to call again. Looking back I had to take my frustration out on someone and she just got in the way that day. Perhaps her phone call was her way of trying to bridge the troubled waters, but at that moment I was not open to her. I am sure she was trying to be nice. "Nice" isn't what we needed. We needed healing.

Windsor followed the baby's father to his workplace one day trying to force him to look at the baby's photograph. He ignored her. Her fury knew no bounds as she created quite a scene. I wanted her to ignore him — move on and let it go. I got more frustrated and angry with her now than when she was pregnant. She was frustrated and angry with me because I wanted to move on. She saw my behavior as uncaring as if I hadn't been affected by the devastating trauma in her life. We couldn't seem to communicate our deepest feelings without a major blow-up.

Eventually she found a young man who promised to fulfill her dreams of a home and family. She declared that this was the one she would marry. His ambition was to ride bulls, for now he was hauling truckloads of hay for a local farmer. He had not finished high school. We tried to give him the benefit of the doubt — we invited him for dinner, tried to get to know him. Our inquiries about his future plans did not reassure us! We knew the story would be the same.

It wasn't long before she was pregnant and he was gone. He didn't want to meet with us to discuss his responsibility. He would not answer the phone and his parents were hostile. As far as he was concerned it was over and he was out the door.

Once again Windsor was faced with betrayal and abandonment. She was doubly angry and wanted revenge. I knew it was futile and tried to get her to focus on her future. But I also knew by now that Windsor would do it her way. I just had to hang on and pray.

Windsor's child's father has not sought custody, visitation or any influence over him. But he has had to pay child-support and medical insurance. At one point, he went to court because he wanted to have his parental rights terminated. When the judge asked if he understood the seriousness of the issue before the court, he said, "Yes, can we get this over fast?" It was incomprehensible to us that not only had he never seen the child but also he was eager to truly abandon all responsibility. When the judge denied the petition, he whined that he just could not afford the child support. Obviously, the judge had heard that line before and ignored his plea.

These two young men broke my child's heart. They abandoned their children. There were times I would have happily broken their necks or boiled them in oil! But God has given me the grace to forgive them and see that they are not are not "bad". They did not encourage, secretly or otherwise, Windsor to terminate the pregnancies. I am grateful for that. On another day, in another situation, I am sure I would have found them to be nice, polite young men. They were young, scared and felt trapped. They saw a way out — they took it. By abandoning Windsor and the child, these young men thought they were taking the easy way out. But they've missed the blessing.

Both babies snuggled into my heart and love knew no bounds! The heartache produced spiritual growth. I have experienced God's grace that I could not have otherwise. "God has made me fruitful in the land of my suffering." (Genesis 41:51)

Sara's Guidance

I have often referred to the men involved in the birth process as suffering from the "Joseph Syndrome", the unfortunate emphasis that we all put on the new mother and baby, forgetting there is also a new father. In the case of unplanned pregnancies, there is also a new father, even though, more often than not he is nowhere to be found. There is also the father of the birthmother who is facing some very hard issues as well. His little girl is having a baby and often he feels as though he didn't protect her enough.

Carey's story....

"I must tell you it took a long time for the anger to go away. The guy who got my daughter pregnant was one of the most self-centered, blood-sucking leaches I have ever had the misfortune of meeting. I wasn't too mad at Anne Marie, but as far as I was concerned death was too good for this pig. Anne Marie was taken in by his charms.

Once I got over my feelings of anger and rage, my feelings about adoption never change from day one. I was always for adoption since I don't believe in abortion and Anne Marie didn't have any money to raise a child and the filthy dog of a father wanted no part of her when he found out she was pregnant. Also, I wasn't about to start over raising children. During the about to start over raising children. During the pregnancy there was a hole in my heart. I knew my daughter would eventually be struggling if she decided to give up the baby, especially when it was time to let her go. My first grandchild was going to be given away to people we barely knew. This cut very deeply into my heart. I sure didn't want to start my grand parenting like this.

As the pregnancy went on, it kept getting harder and harder on everyone involved. The days to the baby's delivery grew closer and closer and I was sickened by the fact that my younger than she should be, pregnant daughter had to make a decision that I, myself was not sure I would be capable of making. The only consolation was knowing the adoptive parents were good Christian people and wanted to love this child.

Dana was born and just as her counselor had told us, Anne-Marie changed her mind after the birth and insisted she would keep the baby. This threw everyone into turmoil. By using reasoning and kindness her mother and I talked her out of keeping the baby. I never remember seeing more pain in my daughter's face, before or since the moment she handed the baby over to her adoptive parents.

Life since Dana was born, nearly seven years ago, hasn't been nearly as bad as I thought it was going to be. The adoptive parents have corresponded with us on a regular basis and sent us pictures of Dana every

year. Recently, my wife Anne, got a surprise when Dana
herself wrote, "Dear Grandmom Pierce" I think Anne
was overwhelmed with joy and panic at the same time."

In unplanned pregnancies, it is unusual for the birthfather to take an active role in the birth and decision making process for the child. Most deny even being the father and if they do admit to it, they will usually tell the mother, "Do whatever you want", abdicating all responsibility. We sometimes refer to these men as sperm donors, since the title "father" implies something they are not. If you are fortunate enough to have the baby's father actively involved, keep him involved, regardless of your personal feeling for him at this point This is his child and believe it or not, he has feelings too, they are just different from ours.

I know this is my child, but it doesn't seem fair
that all of the important decisions are being made
without me being asked. I know she has a harder job,
but I am the father. — Bill

Most young men tend to feel they and their opinions are not wanted or needed in pregnancy related issues, which would include adoption, abortion or parenting. It is true that a woman can abort her child without the permission of the father, but she cannot release the baby for adoption without his cooperation. And of course, if she decides to parent the child, the father will be financially responsible until the child is eighteen.

As a society, we tend to overlook the role of fathers in the lives of our children, but the single most important factor in a young woman's relationship with men in her life, is her relationship with her father. Fathers are extremely important in the lives of our sons and daughters. The following are just a few statistics that show how fatherlessness affects children.

- Children from fatherless homes are 20 times more likely to end up in jail
- 90% of runaway children are from fatherless homes
- 71% of teenage pregnancies are to children of single parents

So, to all of you men out there reading this book, whether you are the birthfather, grandfather or just an interested young man, you are a very important part of the life of your child and don't let anyone tell you differently. Your sons will want to be like you and your daughters will compare every man they ever date to you, so keep this in mind as you decide the course of your life. Fathers teach their children things mothers can't, how to be a man and how to love and treat a woman. Fathers give the home a feeling of safety, like nothing bad will ever happen while dad is home. The sound of his strong, firm voice lets us know that there is someone protecting us from the world. Fathers, you are extremely important in the lives of your children, please don't forget that.

Chapter 7 — To Do List

The Man's Side

Birthfather

- Remember, you are in this together
- Listen to each other
- Respect each other's feelings
- Know your legal rights
- Face your actions with honesty
- Find a man you respect and get his counsel

Support Network

- Love them
- Support their decision
- Listen to them
- Forgive them
- Don't condemn

Finding The Perfect Family

Ruth's Story — A Mother's Heart

Things were not going well for Windsor. The home for unwed mothers where she was staying was not a good fit. I was worried about this as I drove to Philadelphia. A friend, Sara Dormon, in Philadelphia had arranged a surprise birthday for two mutual friends and I drove up from Virginia to be part of the surprise. Another friend flew in from Atlanta.

I have known these ladies for a long time. We get together several times a year for lunch. We laugh, cry, and talk about current issues and books. We share with one another our thoughts, concerns — lives. We are all of different ages and backgrounds but we have a deep bond that transcends our differences. I have always found this group to be loving wise and understanding.

During the luncheon I confided in them about Windsor's situation knowing Sara provided a home, counseling, advocacy and support for women in crisis pregnancies, facilitated their decision process to parent or adopt. With expertise, she was able to ask me direct questions and give helpful suggestions. During our time together that day, the friend from Atlanta, who is very discerning, made the comment that Windsor's baby was going to be a special child and that God had his hand on it. I appreciated her words but did not think much more about it.

I drove home to Virginia feeling encouraged until Windsor called to tell me how unhappy she was. She was homesick and miserable.

If Windsor ain't happy, nobody's happy!

My heart was heavy. She was not cooperating with the program there and felt that they were "programming" her to release the baby for adoption. She resisted this and did not want anyone telling her what she should do — she was going to make her own decision!

Unbeknownst to me, the day of the Philadelphia luncheon, my friend from Atlanta told Sara of a young couple in her church Bible study group, the Nelsons, that had been trying to have a child but had been disappointed. Sara suggested that they send a profile to her. They did and Sara filed it away.

My phone rang later that week and it was Sara on the other end asking if I would consider sending Windsor to live with her. She and her family were willing to take Windsor into their home. Sara would home school her so Windsor would not lose academic ground. She would personally walk Windsor through the decision process of parenting or releasing so that Windsor could make the decision that was best for her baby. Sara knew far better than I all the issues and emotions involved.

As a tough lady with a tender heart for young women like Windsor, Sara would be a good match for Windsor! I could not believe the gift that was being offered so graciously. I didn't even pray about it! I knew this would be a good place for Windsor.

I called Windsor and told her about the offer. I think she saw this as a way out of where she was and as a chance to come back home. Initially, she wasn't committed to going to Philadelphia. When I explained who Sara was and what the requirements would be, after many phone calls, Windsor agreed to meet her.

My husband and I drove Windsor to Philadelphia. And while I knew this was the best possible solution, I had to let it be Windsor's decision or she would have resisted at every turn. I did put pressure on her, however, and she knew that we were out of options. In the end, she agreed to stay with the Dormons. I hated to drive away, leaving her in another new situation. How many changes had Windsor already been through?

It was a bumpy ride.

Over the weeks, Sara walked her through the realities of parenting and adoption. Windsor vacillated daily between parenting and releasing. It tested every level of patience and sanity. She began to talk about adoption and wanted to look at profiles that Sara had of couples wishing to adopt.

The file of prospective adopting couples included the profile of the Nelsons. Once Windsor saw their picture and read their profile, she wanted to meet them. Cheryl is a special education teacher and Eric is a lawyer. Windsor related to them because she had always had difficulty in school and needed extra tutoring. Since she could argue the legs off a table, we had always teased her that she would make a good lawyer.

Sara made arrangements for the Nelsons to come to Philadelphia. I drove up from Virginia. I was nervous to meet them — would they like us? How did you meet someone interested in adopting your flesh and blood? What do you say? What do you talk about? I am sure they were as nervous, maybe more so, than we were. I found them to be delightful and I liked them as people. I would have chosen them as friends and concluded that they were a stable and strong couple. I was concerned about how they would respond to the fact that the baby they would adopt was Billy Graham's great-grandchild. Would it change things? I closely watched their reaction to the news. They didn't flinch and it changed nothing. If Windsor decided to release her baby to this couple, then they would be in our family but not of it. They would hold a unique and special place in our lives.

Windsor asked many questions and told them that at the time, she was still undecided. It was an agonizing decision and we needed time to come to terms with all the implications.

Sara's Guidance

When you think about the family you want your child to live with, make a dream list, as long as you want, with all the qualities of the "perfect family". You must first realize that even though you are seeking the "perfect" family for your child, there aren't any out there. There is however, a *perfect* family to raise your child. On this list should be things like: they have children, or not, they live in the city/suburbs, they have pets, they go to church, the mother works or not. Include anything that you feel is important. As you make this list, keep in mind the decision you are making will impact the rest of your child's life. It is an extremely important decision and should be made carefully. The list is something you can do alone or with the birthfather if he is involved, but you should eventually discuss this list with your support network, especially your mother. She has been a parent and raised a child and she knows what is important. Once you have finished your list, go back and put a check beside those things that are non-negotiable. Usually the single most important quality for you will be having a full-time, stay at home mom. This doesn't mean she will never leave the house until your child walks down the aisle, it means your child will have a full time mother for the most important time and years of his/her life. It means your child will not be put into daycare while the adoptive mother's career can be fulfilled. Incidentally, in my experience, women trying to adopt are more than ready to stay home and be a full time mother.

Once you have your list, you need to decide what type of adoption would best meet your needs. There are open adoptions and the degree of openness varies considerably. There are closed adoptions, which means you may or may not have a lot of say in the amount of information you receive about prospective families. The single most important thing for you to remember is that this is *your* child, *your* decision and *you* are in control of the outcome. Obviously, the birthfather has the same rights you do, but usually he will go along with anything you want. This doesn't give you the right to be unreasonable in your requests, it just means that you have every right to express your wishes and desires and if necessary, negotiate with the adoptive parents.

In the adoptions being done today, the majority of them are open. This means you will meet the prospective couples you are interested in considering as parents. You will be able to ask them questions and they will ask questions of you. If you wish, they can be present at the birth.

They can and will be as involved as you want them to be. Once they have your child in their care, they will send you pictures, letters and even an occasional phone call. This goes on, in some cases, indefinitely. These issues are things you need to discuss with your counselor, parents, and birthfather.

In a closed adoption, it is just that, closed. You would not have the opportunity to choose the parents, you would know very little about them and they in turn would know very little about you. Contact after the fact would be minimal and there would be a lot of unanswered questions on both sides. Some young women do choose closed adoption, mostly as a means to act as if the whole experience has never happened. My personal and professional experience tells me this is not the healthiest approach. These girls will and should need to talk about this experience, and if no one close to them knows what they have done, they have closed that door to healing.

There are several ways to find profiles of couples wanting to adopt. Couples can be found through an adoption agency, through an attorney, or through an adoption facilitator. Adoption agencies can be found in the yellow pages, online or through recommendations. There is an American Academy of Adoption Attorneys that specializes in adoption. These are the attorneys you should use. It is extremely important to have an attorney who knows adoption law. It is a very complicated specialty and requires the expertise of a specialist. Some states do not allow facilitators to take part in the adoption process, so it is very important to know the laws of your state. If you opt for an open adoption and work with a facilitator, you can look at as many profiles as you wish. In the appendix, we have included an example of what a profile will look like. You will look at profiles that most closely match the list of "perfect" family qualities you have written. These profiles are meant to tell you just enough about the couple to get your interest in wanting to know more about them. As an experienced facilitator, I recommend that you look at five or six. Narrowing the list to three or four, you can call or speak with your prospective selections. Once you have talked to the couples and found out more, you will want to have a face-to-face meeting with 2-3. Find a neutral place, like a restaurant or hotel for a meal. The birthfather should be invited to come if he wishes, and your parents, and possibly one other person. The prospective parents don't want to feel ganged up on, and you want the time to be as informative and relaxed as possible

Windsor's Story...

I knew Sara had been working with another girl whose due date was a month before mine. Eventually we met. I was jealous of Cherie because she lived at home, was still in school and the baby's father was still involved. Her life seemed altered very little and reminded me of all the people I felt had walked away from me. One day Cherie came over to go through profiles of couples. She had already made the decision to release her baby for adoption. Once she left, I asked Sara if I could look at the profiles. I think I was curious about these couples: what they looked like, what they did and why they couldn't have children of their own.

I remember as clearly as if it were yesterday. When I opened the files I looked at the first two couples. But when I got to the third couple, I looked hard for some reason and read what they had to say. Staring at the picture, I told Sara that this would be the couple I would pick if I were going to give my baby up for adoption. He was a lawyer and I wanted to be a lawyer. She was a special education teacher, and I have learning difficulties. They were young; he looked like he would be a wonderful dad and they presented themselves in such a way that they really stood out. Without even knowing it, I had just picked the parents for my child.

The goal of this meeting is to learn more about each other. Be prepared to be open, ask questions and they will ask you questions also. As much as you don't want to like them, try to at least be civil. Freely discuss what you want in the way of contact with them and your child. Admittedly, most birthmothers want pictures sent all the time, letters, and the freedom to call at will. This will not be good for you, your child or the adopting parents. We would recommend that you ask for pictures every three months, including letters telling how your child is doing. All adopting parents are willing to do this, some even more. Things such as sending gifts, making phone calls, and possible visits are things that can be discussed as your relationship with the adopting parents develops. Every adopting couple and birthmother are different, so there really isn't a fixed plan for this situation.

Now that you know something about your options, we will discuss feelings, of which you will have many. First of all, nearly anything you feel is all right. Feelings are neutral and they are yours, so don't let anyone tell you, "You shouldn't feel that way." The only thing you need to be careful of is how you handle your emotions. Anger will only hurt you and your child. On the one hand, you will be grateful to the adopting parents, and on the other hand, you will hate them, especially the adoptive mother. She is taking *your place*, and you hate her for it. You won't necessarily act out this anger, nor should you, just be aware you will feel it and it is all right.

Choose parents that come closest to your ideal. Understand that thinking there is no one out there good enough to have my child is normal. As we said before, no one can love your child as much as you do, but there are people who can love your child, just not in the same way. You are that child's mother, for now and forever. Just as you will

ome day find out, you can have more than one child and love them all,
ut your love is different for each child because all children are different.

Cherie's Story...

*I went through the whole process of looking for
an adoptive couple for my baby. I started with a list of
"qualities" that I felt were most important to me, and
that I could not bend on. When looking at different
profiles on prospective adoptive couples, I have to admit
I was a little discouraged and met with several couples
who did not fit the bill. Of course, it is easy to find
something wrong with each couple — why? Because
they are not me, and no one else can be as good a
parent as I would be. Realize that no couple will have
everything, and it is easy to find flaws because they are
not you. I wanted to pick apart every couple so that no
one good existed, and then I could say, "oh well, I
guess I have to keep my baby" — when you know that
may not be the best decision for your baby.*

As I have said before, there are no perfect families or children,
ut you will do the very best you can to find the very best possible
amily for your child. Rely on your instincts and your heart, as well as the
dvice of your support network. Combined, your heart and your instincts
ill let you know who the best family is, trust them.

Chapter 8 — To Do List

Birthparents

- Be realistic
- Accept that no perfect family exists, and look for the best
- Try to get to know them as people
- Ask the adoptive parents to bring pictures, so you can imagine where the baby will live
- Make an effort to find some common ground with the couple

Support Network

- Support the process
- Support her decision
- Support her

9

Letting Go

Ruth's Story — A Mother's Heart

Windsor's plan for releasing the baby was clear: she wanted to take the baby home from the hospital for four days before she released the baby to the Nelsons. I was not sure it was wise. I knew as a mother that it would make the release so much more heart wrenching. But Windsor was insistent, in charge and it was her decision.

In the hospital Windsor vacillated between wanting to keep or release this child. It was a tortured time. We all kept reminding her why she had made the decision to release — called her back to her reasons. Her hormones were out of whack, having just delivered a baby. And her emotions were all over the place. Although I was emotionally exhausted, I had to keep my wits about me.

We took the baby to Sara's home. I watched Windsor's joy for four days while she held her infant daughter and learned to diaper, feed, rock and play. We all bonded with this beautiful baby girl. Family gathered to be introduced to this baby. She was part of us and nestled herself in our hearts.

Because Windsor had decided to release her, I had wanted to protect my heart; I did not want to bond with her. That was no longer possible; this child had moved right in and made herself at home in my heart. Although the time was short, it was wonderful to see Windsor happy with this child. This child was hers, she was beautiful, and it was something Windsor had produced that was perfect.

But our joy turned to anxiety as the day for adoption approached. My own heart was filled with pain and dread. It was like waiting for death — I found myself counting down the days, then hours. The lawyer came over to have the final papers for release signed. The Nelsons took care of the baby in the den while we sat in the dining room. The intense struggle was written all over Windsor's face. I could not push. I only waited until she was ready. I did remind her of the reasons she was releasing the baby.

She cried. She sat staring at the papers. Then she would look at me pleadingly and beg me to let her come home with the baby and help her raise it. She saw her dilemma as my fault and was angry with me. On some levels I was just as angry that she was putting me in this position. After a long time, the papers were signed. I wonder if a State Governor feels the same way as he signs a death sentence for a convicted man.

As we drove to the place for the baptism service and release, tears poured down my cheeks. My heart was breaking, not only for the loss of the baby but also for Windsor. The pain was so intense I was not sure I would make it; I felt that my heart would simply burst. I wanted to run. I wanted to be anywhere else, do anything else but this. And yet, I would not have been anywhere but with my daughter, for her sake.

I was not prepared to watch my child's devastation. Her heart was broken when the young man walked out of her life — taking on none of his responsibility and showing total disregard for her and the baby. Now her heart was shattering; she was releasing the most important thing in her life. It was agonizing to watch. I could not take her pain nor could I protect her from it. Nor could I even fully enter into it. All I managed at that moment was to observe my child in agony while experiencing my own.

We gathered in a friend's living room for the baptism service. Windsor's face was Madonna-like as she cradled her baby close and yet her eyes revealed unspeakable sadness. Windsor looked so beautiful that day, dressed in pink. After the service, we took photographs, passing the baby to each family member. Those photographs reveal so much love and so much pain.

We told Windsor, "It is time." She held the baby that much closer. Windsor smiled bravely for one last photograph with her child. Her eyes, swollen from crying, her heart breaking, she whispered an "I love you" and gently, ever so gently, placed that baby in the waiting arms of the adoptive parents. They got in their car and wept as they drove away.

My child wailed as a new mother who has lost her first and only child. We said hurried goodbyes and got in our car. We headed to Virginia and home. Spent in grief, Windsor slept. But she awoke to an empty womb, an empty heart and empty arms. She faced hours, days, months, years — a lifetime — with part of her heart missing. And she was just 17, a time when those her age are just learning to drive.

I felt like I was coming apart at the seams but I tried to put on a brave face for Windsor. This was a mistake. She wanted, needed to see my pain. She wanted to know that I shared her grief. I was just trying to hold it together. How would we recover? How could we "go on"? Our lives were changed forever. Part of our heart was missing and how can life continue with a piece of your heart missing?

This was grief. Real grief. A death had taken place in our family and now we had to cope.

The retelling of our story is painful. I knew that we had made the best possible decision for the baby. But without a doubt, it was the worst day of my life. And yet, looking back I have never regretted our decisions. Windsor did the right thing — the best thing for her child.

At the time, I could not put two sensible thoughts together. I was exhausted emotionally and physically. I was weary of trying to be wise, gentle and anticipating others' needs and being everything Windsor needed me to be. I had nothing left to give. My husband, Richard, took over. He was focused and strong; we found security in his strength. He didn't say anything as we drove home but he held my hand and let me weep. I caught him looking in the rearview mirror more than once as he checked on Windsor, sleeping.

When she awoke, he engaged her in conversation that was light hearted and focused on the near future. He answered her questions honestly and assured her that he would "be there" for her in the weeks and months to come. He asked her about plans to go to the beach and she wanted to go hiking with him. He included her in all of our outings.

He showed us his love, not in words, but in actions. When advice was called for he offered it with clarity and gentleness. When decisions had to be made he was focused but considerate. When our emotions were raw he was tender. When boundaries were needed, he was consistent but loving. He was sympathetic but never lost perspective. He let us cry and made us laugh. He let us vent but held us tight. I will be forever grateful for his gentle, kind strength.

Let me say to birth-grandfathers, you are important to the process. You provide stability. You need to hold your daughter, put your arms around her. Tell her you love her and do special things with her. Do not shut her out. It may be — it is — awkward for you but you are a very important part of the picture. Don't walk away from her tears. Don't just buy her things — give of yourself. What you do and how you do it can make the difference in how well your daughter puts her life back together. And while you are at it, hold your wife; listen to her.

Sara's Guidance

Having just read Ruth's story about this moment of releasing your child may make you back off of your decision to proceed with adoption. Remember this is okay. You are going to be going through one of the most emotionally wrenching experiences you will ever have to face. You should and have every right to be upset. I don't want to sound mean when I say this, but don't lose sight of the fact that you are in this difficult position of willingly experiencing grief because of choices you made. I say this because you will want to blame everybody, including the mailman, for what you have to deal with right now.

You need to prepare a plan for when, where and how you want to release your child to the adoptive parents. There are as many ways to go about this as there are young women doing it. Just to remind you again, this is your child and while you don't need to make this decision alone, it is yours to make. If the birthfather is involved, of course he should be involved in this decision as well.

Perhaps you have decided that the less time you spend with your child the easier letting go will be. But when the time actually comes to do it, and you have changed your mind, say so. You are in charge and this is your child. Know that spending a lot of time with your baby will make the release harder, but you may be willing to trade the pain for that time. Just remember you are in charge and you have to tell everyone else what you want.

There will be another experience that is going to be very difficult, not that the rest hasn't been. As you heard in Windsor's experience, the lawyer will bring papers that will be used to terminate your parental rights. There will be other papers to sign that allow your child to be able to find you when they turn 18. This process varies by state, which is another reason you should have an adoption attorney advise you, especially if you are a minor. The timing of this will be after the baby is born and you are already an emotional basket case. Be sure you have someone with you when you sign these papers. This should be able to be done in your home or wherever you are living. Remember ask for what you want. There is no preordained time for this to be done, but it shouldn't be put off too long.

We have had many experiences with releasing the child to the adoptive parents, and even those young women who have no strong religious background generally want to have some kind of ceremony. Some women have wanted to be baptized along with their child; others want everyone involved praying over the child. It should be done in a place that is somewhat neutral, without being impersonal. It is extremely important that you are in a place and with people with whom you feel safe. If you have a church home, that is often a good place, but just remember, you are going to have to walk into that church again. For this reason, you should use a room that you would not normally use and an entrance that you won't have to use again. You will relive this time again and again, so it is best to find a place you don't visit often.

Most importantly, take pictures. If videotaping doesn't seem too intrusive, it will be something you will always have. You may want to give your baby a blanket or something your mother may have kept from when you were a child. Virtually anything you want to do at this time, within reason, is all right. Please try to keep in mind that this entire process is emotionally draining for all involved, so it is important to do whatever you can to take care of your self.

If you decide to keep the baby with you for a few days you will not want to sleep. You will want to just hold your baby, watch her sleeping and do whatever you can to have as much time with her as possible. This too is both normal and understandable, but when the time arrives to release her, your hormones and emotions will be so shot you won't be able to function. If necessary, take something to help you relax and sleep.

Just the term letting go hurts to read, we understand that. But rather than focus on the negative aspect of letting go, understand somewhere in your mind that you are doing the very best possible, as well as the most loving, thing you are able to do for your child. You are living out what it means to be a mother.

It may be helpful to actually say "goodbye" out loud while holding your baby, or whenever you choose to say it. It's OK to cry with your baby and let your child hear your voice. This would also be a good time to give your child the letter or journal you have written to them. A letter from you can answer a lot of questions from your child in years to come. If you write a letter, your child will know of your love, that your decision for releasing for adoption was made out of love, not out of not wanting your child. It is likely to be the only message your child might ever have from you and it will be very important to them.

Whenever we lose or let go of something or someone we love, we experience grief. When you release your baby for adoption, you're going to experience the kind of loss and sadness a mother feels when a baby dies. Please be aware that the loss of your baby will be physically and emotionally painful.

You may also find yourself experiencing a sense of grief and relief...grief over the loss and relief that your decision has been made, your pregnancy completed, and your life can get back on track. It is important to note again, that almost any feeling you have in the days following the separation from your child will be normal. Even though you are sure you made the best decision for your child, it hurts and hurting is OK. Grief is a necessary part of this experience and critical to the healing process.

Remember that your body is not only grieving, it is also working to return to an un-pregnant state. You have a lot of hormone changes, weight changes and general body changes happening. Organs that were displaced by the baby are back in their original place and you can finally sleep on your stomach again. You don't have to go to the bathroom every 10 minutes and getting out of a chair can be done without the help of three large men. Any soreness you had, and you will have it, is going away and your milk-filled breasts and returning to their pre-pregnant size. It is more important now than ever before to take good care of yourself. When you get run down physically you will get run down emotionally which will get you run down physically which will get you run down emotionally and so on and so on and so on.

"I was so tired all the time. I thought all I wanted to do was get out of the hospital, start exercising and get my life back to normal. But I couldn't sleep, I ate everything in the refrigerator, and when I watched a sad movie I broke down sobbing." — Julie

While you will physically let go of your child, your baby will live in your heart and mind forever. No matter how much time passes, you will always have the combination of a tear filled smile when you think of your child. Hopefully you will have pictures and letters to document their lives and then one day, when and if they are ready, you will meet again.

The following is a poem written by a birthmother to her baby.

Wish upon a star and your wish may come true.
I wished on a star and they came to take you
Away from my arms, but never my heart
Together nine months, we are now far apart

Don't ever think that I didn't care
I love you, I miss you, in spirit I'm there
And when you are ready, by your side I'll be
Together again, my baby and me.

— Cherie

Chapter 9 — To Do List

Birthparents

- Try to be prepared for one of the most painful, difficult, life-altering events
- Keep focusing on why you are doing this
- Bring your journal and any gifts you have for the baby
- Plan a meaningful, life honoring ceremony

Support Network

- Keep your focus on what's best for the future of the child and the birthparents
- Be there in every way possible
- Acknowledge your own grief, and allow yourself to take the time to grieve
- Acknowledge what she has done, and honor her for the love of her child

10

The Ripple Effect

Noelle's Story

I was a junior at Samford University. Because of my parent's divorce, college was a refuge and, because of my roommate's stable family I enjoyed a "normal" family experience. My academic advisor and his family welcomed me into their lives. I felt blessed. My roommate, Chris, and I had settled into a routine and drew close, like sisters. I loved Windsor dearly and, soon Chris adopted Windsor, too. Windsor would come to visit me at school. She seemed to enjoy my friends. We'd arrange ski trips together where she was included and we talked by phone frequently; often Chris would join in our conversations.

One day, Windsor called me; she said she had something to tell me. Chris could see my expression and knew I was upset so she got on the phone, too. Windsor told me she was pregnant. At age 16!

Our first response was to comfort and reassure Windsor. We wanted her to know we loved her and would be there for her — no matter what. As we hung up the phone, my mind was spinning and I was troubled by the news. As Chris and I talked we said we were not surprised. Windsor's willfulness and inappropriate behavior with boys had seemed to make this inevitable.

I went back to my studies, a true refuge now. I didn't have to think too much about what was going on at home. I knew I didn't have to deal with it everyday. But there were knots in my stomach.

As I said, I loved Windsor — still do. She is my only sister and has looked up to me and, in some ways thought she was in competition with me. She felt she could not measure up to our Dad's expectations. She is my little sister and I love her but there are times I could choke her. I wanted to blast the hell out of her. Hit her over the head but, bottom line was that she was my sister.

Windsor's experience became part of my story, too. It affected our whole family. I became angry at responses like, "Send her to Africa. Let the missionaries take care of her." Or simply ignored her and the situation hoping it would go away. It was as if they were pretending nothing was wrong. Graham, our brother, Windsor and I had gone through the devastation of divorce and, now were dealing with this pregnancy. Where were the ones we needed most? Could they not practice what they preached? I felt as if we were the black sheep of the family. No longer loved quite the same — we weren't "perfect". I was left bewildered and angry, especially for Windsor's sake. But gradually, I came to realize that we are as sinful as all the rest.

On top of this my mother got married again! This was too much. I had always loved Richard and welcomed him into our family, but I was trying to adjust to so many things all at once.

I agreed that Windsor was not ready to raise a child and that adoption was her best option. I supported her and loved her. I had met the adopting couple and liked them very much. I thought Windsor had made a wise choice and that the baby would have a wonderful home.

I spent six weeks of the summer in Rwanda working with orphans. I hadn't been home with Windsor, but had had a great experience and, came home to the imminent birth of Windsor's baby. I wanted to talk about my experiences, show my photographs. Mom wasn't home; she was in Philadelphia with Windsor. So I got in my car and drove to Philadelphia to "deal with Windsor". My brother had flown in from Dallas so we were all there. No one was particularly interested in my African experience — at least not at the time.

I had steeled my heart for the baby's birth. I knew she was to be released so did not anticipate allowing this child to gain entry into my heart. Windsor did give birth to a baby girl early on July 25th. We all piled into her room the next morning to be with her and see the baby she had named Victoria Windsor.

What a beautiful baby, so petite — with a head full of hair. We all fell in love. Head over heels. The child was no longer Windsor's but ours. I now wanted to keep her and, could only imagine how torn Windsor must have been at the idea of giving Victoria over to some other woman. And Windsor did vacillate! Boy! did she ever and, it created turmoil. We all had to keep reminding ourselves that the decision Windsor had made months ago when emotions were not so high was still the right decision.

The time arrived to release the baby. It was a very emotional time. I cried, as we all did. I was concerned for my parents, and the heartache they were enduring. It is hard to see your parents distraught and you can do nothing to make it better. I was angry about everything. I threw myself into exercise, working out twice a day and, engaging my eating disorder like a long lost friend.

I was looking forward to going back to college where I didn't have to deal with this every day. I could leave it behind. Because I was the oldest I felt responsible and carried the burdens of my brother and sister. Most of the time they didn't much care whether I did or not.

Windsor was harder on herself than anyone else. She was expressing shame and remorse. I included Windsor in most of my activities and, enjoyed her in a whole new way. She was compliant, thoughtful, her joy had come back and, I welcomed this Windsor with delight. For the rest of the summer we had peace in the house. Yes, we talked about Victoria — often. Yes, we looked at the photos and the videos sent by the adoptive parents. I hoped and prayed that we were moving on and healing.

The deadline for finalization of the adoption came. Windsor had vacillated and, at the last minute called the adoptive couple to bring Victoria back. She couldn't go through with the adoption. Talk about emotions! I was angry that she had waited until the last minute. I was furious at her for putting our family though this, not to mention what she was doing to the young couple. They had had Victoria for a full month. They were bonded to her! How could Windsor do this? This is one of the times I wanted to choke her.

She settled down, the adoption did happen and, we made plans to move on. I went back to Samford University. Windsor was looking forward to joining her senior class at the local high school.

It would prove to be a bumpy ride. I was glad to be out of the center of the storm. As soon as she got back to school Windsor began to run with the wrong crowd and eventually left home to bounce from house to house — none of them good. I became angry for what she was putting Mom and Richard through. After all they had done to support her, how could she do this to them — to all of us?

During that year she came to visit me. Chris and I tried to talk some sense into her. In May, the family gathered in Washington to participate in my Grandparent's receiving of the Congressional Medal of Honor in the Capital Rotunda. Later in May we all gathered for Windsor's graduation.

Too soon Windsor revealed she was pregnant — again. My reaction was to be angry. She had been given so much. It was like she had traded her inheritance for something cheap, unsatisfying. The hardest part was that she had settled for crumbs when she could have had the whole cake! I was confronted with a choice. I could abandon Windsor with conditional love or I could model for her forgiveness and unconditional love. I chose the later because I love Windsor; she is my little sister.

Our pride that she had been able to complete high school on time with her class was subdued by our knowledge that she was pregnant under her robe. But I loved her and would support her through it again.

Windsor went to summer school anticipating entry into college. went back to Samford. Mom and Richard got Windsor settled into a little apartment near her college and, she began classes. Members of the faculty were very helpful and kind to Windsor. I was hoping she would love college and begin to form a future for herself.

Her due date was near Thanksgiving and the baby arrived Thanksgiving week. Mom and Richard were with her at the birth. Well, not Richard, he waited in the hall. He gets very agitated when he sees someone he loves in pain and, is unable to do anything about it. Windsor called me to tell me she had given birth to a little boy: Walker Wyatt Dienert.

Mom drove them home for Thanksgiving and we all got to meet Walker. Windsor had vacillated about whether or not to also release this baby to the same adoptive parents. She was going to try to parent him and, after Thanksgiving Mom and Richard took Windsor and Walker back to school to finish the semester.

She decided to parent Walker. She could not go through another release of her child. I could understand far better this time but wondered if she would be a good mother. Could she raise this child by herself? I began to wonder if I should raise Walker myself. I was finishing college and felt Windsor was unstable and I could give Walker more stability than she could. Mom had told her she couldn't live at home but had to live elsewhere. She decided to go live with Dad in Dallas for a short while. She missed her friends so wanted to return. Mom still would not allow her to live at home. I felt sorry for Windsor but also knew my Mom could not handle parenting Windsor while she attempted to parent Walker.

Eventually, Windsor went back to Philadelphia to live. She's a good mother and Walker is a delightful little boy. I would not trade him for anything! As he gets older, with each passing year he worms himself into my heart and I find enormous pleasure in being an aunt. I have so much fun with him. He loves to come for overnight visits. I am teaching him how to ride a horse. My husband, Maury, has embraced Walker, too. We both love Windsor and Walker.

Windsor and I have grown closer and while she is still my little sister and there are times I want to choke her, I am sure there are times she wants to choke me. Things are pretty much back to normal except now we have the joy of Walker!

Sara's Guidance

When you begin this journey, you will be convinced that no one but you is as scared, sad, angry or hurting. That is not true. Those in your support network are experiencing the same emotions you are, just not with the same intensity or as often. To you it will seem as though their lives have not changed, but remember, everybody deals with crises in different ways. Just as a stone is thrown into a pond and the ripples are generated from there to the shore, so is the effect of an unplanned pregnancy. The stone is the pregnant woman and from her, every one of those her life touches, will be affected by this pregnancy and the decisions that follow. Even if some of these people don't do or say the right thing, or anything at all, that is fine. Give them the time they need to process the information and decide how they see themselves fitting into the picture. Some won't want to fit in at all, and that choice has to be respected, not liked, but respected.

You will want everybody, especially the baby's father to hurt as much as you do. He can't, for a lot of reasons. For one, he is a man and men are not able to have the same connection and feelings that you have with your child. They will never feel a baby move inside them and never experience the pain of bringing it into the world. Women were created and designed intellectually, physically, emotionally and spiritually for this very thing. So rather than waste a lot of energy being angry at him, try to bring him into the experience as much as you can by including him in as many of the decisions as he wants to be included.

Remember that this child is the grandchild of his parents as well as your parents. Lean on him in any and all ways he will let you.

A crisis pregnancy affects everyone in your circle of influence: your parents, the birthfather's parents, siblings on both sides, grandparents, close friends of yours and your families, co-workers of all of the above. This is the "ripple effect".

Cherie's Story...

It affects your family, as I said before, more than you could imagine. I remember a year or so after my son was born. I was upset and screaming at my mother." You made me give away my baby", or some false statement like that, knowing full well that she would've been pleased as punch if that baby came home with us. It was entirely my decision to release him for adoption. And to my surprise my mother yelled back at me (which, by the way, she seldom does — ever). She screamed," Let me tell you how I hurt because you gave away my grandbaby!"

OOHHHH NO!! I thought she didn't just say that. But it helped me to realize how I gave away their grandbaby and she must've hurt about that too. It was a great reality check. This whole year she has to had been hurt about that and I didn't know it until then. She stayed up the night I had him and as I slept she went to the nursery and got the baby and just rocked him all night. In addition, after our "release" ceremony my sister, with whom I had been fighting for years, turned to my mother and said "Can't we just take him home?" Wow — I hurt her too — she loved her nephew too and it tore her up inside to see him go.

This is just one example of how one moment in time, nine months earlier, can have an everlasting effect on many people in our lives. Some of those who are affected we may never know about. But be assured, this experience does and will have a ripple effect, the only question is how far does that ripple reaches.

During one of the many release ceremonies I was involved in, the baby was being prayed over by the birthparents before handing it over to the adoptive parents. I watched the youngest sister of the birthmother gasp for breath as she sobbed. She understood why her sister was making the choice and she loved the adoptive family, but this was her niece, her big sisters' baby, and a member of her family. She felt, "How could anyone give away a member of their family?" But that is exactly what her sister was doing and it hurt her immensely.

Try to allow all those in your support network know that you are aware of the fact that this is an experience for which there is no preparation. They need to be given permission, by you, to be able to express their grief in whatever way they choose. Experiencing grief is good and healthy and we must not try and take it from them, nor should we allow others to take it from us. This is what is called good and healing grief.

Chapter 10 — To Do List

Birthparents

- Be aware that others hurt too
- Don't expect the birthfather to feel the way you do
- Others will not know what to do or say to you — that doesn't mean that they do not care, they do, they just don't know how to express it
- Accept that there will be a lot of unspoken thoughts and feelings

Support Network

- Acknowledge how this has affected you
- Listen to all involved
- Don't assume how they feel

11

I Don't Fit In

Ruth's Story — A Mother's Heart

How do you move on and fit in? How do you relate to others — riends? family? church members? This was more uncharted territory for us.

We arrived back in Virginia at loose ends not knowing where to begin. What do you do the day after you release a child for adoption? I wanted to get life back to normal; but it never would be. My emotions were spent. I was exhausted. A piece of my heart was missing.

I felt my daughter needed me to provide some sense of routine. The world had not come to an end and there were things that needed to be done: meals to cook, groceries to buy, mail to catch up on, phone calls to return — the familiar things that I thought would bring some order back into our lives. She resented it but it was the only way I knew to cope.

A few of my female friends had a shower for Windsor. By doing this they weren't ignoring what had happened. They were interested in seeing the pictures of the baby and letting her tell her story. They gave her a luncheon and presented her with gifts for herself. They offered her opportunities to learn how to make things with her hands. They gave her gift certificates for beauty treatments. They asked questions about her future plans and ideas. It was a lovely thing for them to do. I will be forever grateful.

Others remained quiet. And silence is usually perceived negatively in such a situation. Many, perhaps most people, did not know what to say or do and did not inquire as to what would be appropriate. They assumed "to do nothing is better than to do the wrong thing". I cannot describe my guilt and self-condemnation, and my shame as those who had daughters who were not pregnant would ask about Windsor. They didn't intend to make me feel like a failure — but they did. I thought "failure" had been tattooed on my forehead for all to see.

My church friends and acquaintances didn't do much better. They didn't know what to say, so they, too, remained silent. When they sought to help it was as if my raw emotions and fragile self-esteem had been trampled by combat boots. The kind of help they offered was conditional and rigid. Their answers were pat answers. They did not get in the trenches with us and "bear our burden". It was as if they were on the sidelines shouting instructions from a safe distance. Their compassion was conditioned on her attitude of remorse. The comfort offered was short lived — they were busy, they had to move on to the next "problem". The church leaders told me that after all I was Billy Graham's daughter and had lots of resources!

Where was the church? Why had it not stood in the gap for us? Why had they ignored our dilemma and us? Our immediate family was the only support network she had and we were stretched very thin.

I was expressing to a pastor how Windsor wanted to be congratulated as a mother; she had carried a child beneath her heart for nine months and had given birth. She then voluntarily gave that baby to another woman. She wanted some measure of recognition for that act of love. The circumstances of this birth did not diminish the fact that the life — her baby — was a miracle. The pastor was adamant that she should not expect to be congratulated or treated as a legitimate mother since her child had been born out of wedlock and released for adoption. I tried to understand his viewpoint but in my mind, it conflicted with what I believed Jesus had called the church to do.

It is God's job to convict of sin and produce repentance. The church was established to be a channel of God's grace and wisdom. It was to equip the saints to minister not only to those outside the church but those inside it. The church is to act as Jesus would — it is His arms, legs, and face. Jesus, himself, was born under a cloud of suspicious parentage. Certainly, he understood.

Do you congratulate a birthmother? Yes. She carried a baby to term and went though labor and delivery. She is a mother. When does a woman become a mother? When she decides to put the needs of her child above her own needs. When does the adoptive mother become a legitimate mother? When she chooses to care for that child, putting its needs above her own.

Do you send flowers and balloons to a birthmother? Yes. One of Sara's sons, who had become like a brother to Windsor, gave her a balloon that said, "Way to Go!" Does this overlook the fact that this child is "illegitimate"? I don't like labels and no child is a mistake. The child may have come out of "proper" sequence, but it is a blessing.

To explain this further, I recently heard a story of a couple in the Midwest who found out their sixteen year old was having a baby out of wedlock. Heartbroken, they went to their pastor. When they told him he responded, "Isn't that wonderful!" They were nonplussed and confused by such response. What could he mean? He told them that one day that "problem", that "mistake", would wrapped its little arms around them and squeeze their necks. He said, "All your problems should turn out that way." What a great insight by a very wise pastor!

After Windsor had released her child in late July, for the remainder of the summer, she settled down and was delightful company. She stuck pretty close to home and we tried to do special things with her, including her in all of our activities. She went with us to the beach and I remember catching her watching "trash TV" more than once. The people on those shows had problems that made Windsor's life seem like a walk in the park! Windsor didn't want to go to church because it made her feel like a "scarlet woman".

She wanted to go back to her public high school in September — that had been the plan all along. It had been her goal in keeping up with her academic work so that she would be able to graduate with her class. But Windsor did not fit in. She was no longer a teenager. Her friends were incredulous that she "gave her baby away". They ostracized her for her decision. Their comments and questions were cruel creating more pain and self-doubt. She could not relate to them, nor they to her. The "good kids" didn't want her around for fear she would drag them down — she would be a bad influence. The youth leaders at church didn't know what to do for her either; they had no training in this area, so they did nothing. She was a "hot potato". Windsor gravitated towards those who didn't make her feel so badly about herself, those who had made the same or even worse choices.

I watched in agony as she began a self-destructive, downward spiral as she created sorrow upon sorrow for herself and others. She began to date again and these young men were only interested in one thing. Windsor was desperately looking for love — someone to make her feel whole again. Things deteriorated rapidly. My husband and I told Windsor that if she didn't live by our rules she would have to move out. She was unwilling to cooperate and decided to leave.

That was a wrenching experience for us. I knew the danger of what she was doing. I hated it. I knew she would regret her actions. I begged her to reconsider. She was spinning out of control. She moved in with a variety of people and at one point, I asked the police to help me extricate her from one place. She became very angry and verbally abusive with me and all of her family.

Her behavior indicated to us she was keeping her pain at bay. I understood that and it hurt at levels I did not know I had. It was as if my child was drowning and I could only watch from the shore, running back and forth, screaming for help but no one could hear me. This went on for almost a year.

In May, she informed my husband she was pregnant again. When he told me, I cried; I could not go through it again. I told her she was on her own. She went to a counselor who was doing all he could to help her see the destructive patterns in her life. We spent hours in his office. Eventually he was instrumental in getting her to apply and be accepted into college. We all wanted her to have goals and see that there was life beyond the hurt.

That summer she spent two months back in Philadelphia with Sara. Although I had said she was on her own, I could not abandon her. In September we moved her into a small apartment at the college and she did well in her studies. The college was wonderful to her and did all they could to help her succeed. In November, she gave birth to a little boy. It was Thanksgiving and I brought them home for the weekend. She did not know whether she would also release this child for adoption or parent him herself. If she released him, she wanted the Nelsons to have him. When she asked them, they were willing.

That Thanksgiving weekend as she attempted to nurse him, trying so hard to be a good mother, I felt pity for her. Although she desperately wanted to keep him, I felt that the odds against this going well were just too great. She had never had much patience so I worried when he would cry too long. As I looked down the road, I asked myself how would she support him, care for him?

My heart was guarded; I was detached from this little boy. He was a dear little thing but I would not let him in. My own anger with Windsor blocked this relationship. I was angry that this had happened again, I felt she had taken advantage of our love for her. She had run roughshod over my heart. Not just once, or twice, but over and over again.

She did not go back to college and I told her she could not live with me. I would not take on her responsibilities. Her father, who lived in Dallas, told her she could live with him. She went down at Christmas time and stayed.

She vacillated between releasing and parenting. Eventually she called Sara saying she just couldn't possibly parent this baby and wanted to come home to Virginia to make her final decision. No one thought it was a good idea. I was afraid of the influence of her friends and that she might try to contact the father. I planned to keep her under "house arrest". Against everyone's better judgment, she came home. It wasn't long before her friends were showing up ay my door and the phone line was tied up late into the night.

Sara had put us in touch with a lawyer in Virginia who drew up adoption papers for this child. The day we were to drive to Richmond, I had to speak at a local Rotary Club luncheon. It was surreal. When I got back from the luncheon the three of us got in my car and headed for Richmond. Every few miles, she would tell me to turn around, she couldn't go through with this.

I wanted to arrive after the baby's father had left the lawyer's office so that Windsor would not have to confront him. Unfortunately my timing was a few minutes off. She was told that the father was in the next office; she went ballistic! This young man had walked away from her and his child with not so much as a look backwards though he had promised marriage and his parents had told the young couple they could live with them. So many broken promises...I understood her anger. I was angry with him, too.

But she had to calm down so she could think. She stared at the papers. She told me she couldn't do it. I kept asking her what she thought was best for her child. She stared some more. After over an hour she signed the papers with a mix of heartbreak and anger. She felt trapped, but the lawyer assured her that she had thirty days to change her mind.

We drove home. Windsor called the Nelson's to tell them that the papers were signed and they could come pick up the baby. Plans were made. Windsor was full of indecision as the days passed. Rather than having her decision confirmed, her doubts multiplied. I just tried to stay on course. One hour she was going to parent the baby, the next she wasn't. It was a roller coaster of emotion.

The Nelson's were due the next day. I was down in my office working on an assignment for my class when Windsor came in with her news. She had called the Nelsons, reaching them as they were walking out the door. She told them not to come because she had decided she wanted to keep her son.

I remember being quite resigned when she told me. This had been her decision to make. I got up, hugged her and told her that I was glad she was settled with it and now could move forward. In my heart, I felt genuinely sad for the Nelsons' in their disappointment.

When Windsor left the room, I picked up my Bible and my eyes fell on the verse, "The earth is the Lord's and all they that dwell therein." (Psalms 24:1) I felt that meant that Windsor and Walker, her baby boy, belonged to God and he loved them more than I did. He would take care of them. I had an unexplained peace in my heart that could only come from God.

Sara's Guidance

You have just given birth, spent three days with your new baby, placed the child in the arms of someone who will take the child home to raise and love. You've been through levels of loss and grief others will probably never experience. Now you are going to return to your senior year in high school and listen to your friends talk about their boyfriends, cheerleading, football games and the teachers they don't like. Somehow, this all seemed so much more important last year than it does now. How can comparing nail polish colors compare with such a life-altering experience?

All you want to do is scream and say, "Do you people have any idea of what I have just gone through?" The answer is "no", and they never will. This is an unfortunate, but very real part of your life. You just won't fit in where you used to and part of you doesn't want to. Even if you feel as though you do, at least on the surface, deep down inside you have been profoundly changed forever. Yes, you are still a young and beautiful, but now you must add to that description the word "mother". That puts you in a unique category with much older women. But, by releasing your child for adoption your uniqueness becomes even greater.

It will take time for you to find that place where you will feel comfortable relating to your peers. Some peers may not wish to relate to you, but it is important to make an effort to find a balance of friends in your life again. You may find that because of your experience certain people may be attracted to you and others won't. Try and be aware of what their motives may be and protect yourself. Some people will understand your decision, but most won't. Don't feel the need to try and explain your life, but know that for those who want to hear, your experience will hold treasures. Their experience in life has been limited and things that were important to you nine months ago, aren't important anymore, or not as important. That is all right. You may find yourself overcome with unexplained emotions at unexpected times. You will have a grief and sadness that will be so deep, sometimes you will feel like you are going to cave in and die. All of this is not only normal, but should be expected. Your need for counseling may be even more important now, as well as being part of a support group.

Having on going counseling to deal with these and a lot of other surfacing emotions over the next few years is a good thing. This doesn't mean you should be in counseling long term, but you should be in it as long as you feel the need to be there. Finding a birthmother support group where you will have women who share your experience and with whom you can talk is the best advice I can give. This helps you realize that almost everything you are feeling is not only normal, but also that the other women are going through the same thing. It also helps to meet women who have gone through this and not only survived, but also thrived.

Your relationship with your mother will also change. You now know what she went through to have you. Remember what we said earlier. Your mother has gone through the same experience, but from a different vantage point. Her response to your issues may be different from yours. Different is acceptable. Please don't mistake "different" for not caring. Your mother has lost her grandchild, her child's child. It is no small thing. Tension and anger will reside under the surface of your lives. You will at times feel as though you were forced into releasing you child and feel anger toward your mother because of this. You know your mother loves you so you will feel safe venting your anger on her. You know she can and will take it, all the time loving you, hurting with you, and desperately wanting to take your pain away. Make it a goal to love your family.

Cherie's Story...

I don't fit. I definitely had some issues once I got back to a normal routine after having the baby. Whether it was going back to school, or moving back home, I felt like I could no longer relate to my same friends as I had done just nine months before. I felt like I had just done something so great by giving my baby life. What an enormous task that is. Others would not be able to understand that for years. All my friends talked about were boys and what party was going on and who was dating whom. Having made a defining decision affecting another life, your child's', it's as if these things I used to have in common with my friends now seem so unimportant, almost trivial. I realized I had matured far beyond my years. Going back to their level felt like regressing.

I am not saying go out and get new friends who are "grown-ups". I am saying, that once you start hanging out again you will come to a happy medium that works for you. As far as what activities you may still like and which friends you can tolerate and which ones still have their heads in the clouds and have no clue as

*to how much bigger the world is outside of them you
will also find your balance there and spend your time
with those people who will encourage and edify you. It
will never be the same because you cannot erase the
past nine months, what you have been through and the
fact that you are a mother. But you have had this
experience and now can take from it a wealth of
knowledge. See what you can apply from it to help
others and to help yourself not to make the same
mistake again.*

Along with not fitting in, you will face certain situations after you release your child that you can try and prepare for, but more often than not, when they do happen it will come as a big surprise. These include anniversaries, photographs, new names and reunions.

Anniversaries

Every month, for the first year, on the date of the child's birth, most birthmothers relive the experience. This is somewhat true for all mothers, but your situation is different. Because of your decision to release your child for adoption, you are not able to celebrate in the same way other mothers do. Consequently, the anniversary of your child's birth will be filled with grief and pain as opposed to joy and laughter. This will not last forever and does diminish over time. Hopefully, you will have agreed with the adoptive parents to allow you to send a gift on the first birthday and subsequent birthdays. If not, for whatever reason, on your child's birthday, do something special for yourself to commemorate the value of what you have done by giving life.

Also, when Mothers' Day comes around, you are going to feel as though someone has pulled your heart out, ground it up into small pieces, and shoved it back into your chest. Every sign, card, and TV commercial that refers to Mother's Day will make you feel as though someone is pouring salt onto your wounded heart. It is very important to you to be recognized as a mother, but you need to tell people that this is the case. Don't get angry with people for not doing something when they don't know what is appropriate to do or what you want them to do. Tell them what you need.

Pictures

You will be getting pictures of your child based on whatever frequency you have agreed to with the adoptive parents. Beware! Usually you will get the first pictures within the first three months. When you get these pictures you will see a child that will not look like the child you held in your arms. The pictures themselves may have your child in the arms of "That woman!" This will hurt, and as much as it hurts, it is just one part of the reality you have chosen and the reality you are offering your child. You will have to learn to live with this knowing time heals.

You will feel as though this is not your child at all now. They not only look different, but the name is different from the one you gave them. They will grow and change; at some point you will receive a picture and it will seem as though you are looking at a total stranger. In many ways you are, but again, you are and always will be your child's mother.

The Name

We strongly recommend that you give your child a name of your choosing. You will have the chance to fill out forms in the hospital to get an original birth certificate with your name and your child's name on it. We would encourage you to do this. You can put this, your hospital nametag, cards, anything you want in a scrapbook. Also, you should know that the adopting couple may or may not choose to use the name you have chosen. Every birthmother wants every adopting couple to use the name she chose. Some may, and some will use part of the name, but some may not want to use any of it. As much as this will hurt, this is part of the process of healing. More often than not, the adoptive parents will refer to your child by the name you gave her, but after a while you need to tell them they can use the name they have chosen. It doesn't change anything and is really only your way of keeping her as a part of you as long as possible. You will always refer to your child by the name you have given. Again, you will always be this child's mother, now and forever.

Reunions

Meeting your child may or may not happen, but you need to prepare for it. We don't recommend visiting your child, especially early on. It would be like ripping a scab off of a healing wound. At the time of release, you will be asked to sign a paper as to whether or not you want your child to be able to contact you when the child turns 18. Just signing "yes" to this, does not guarantee it will happen. It merely means you are giving the court permission to allow your child the opportunity to contact you. One advantage in an open adoption is that you will have ongoing contact with the adoptive family, so neither you nor your child will have to hunt the other down. Because you will know where your child is, you will be tempted to want to initiate the reunion. Don't!! A successful reunion can only take place when both parties want it to happen and this should be when the child is capable of handling a mature event. Assuming you will always want it to occur, have the presence of mind and heart to allow your child to come to you. Also, be aware of the possibility that as you mature, get married, have a family, *you* may not want to have this reunion. You need to allow that your feelings may change. You won't believe that now, but don't rule out the possibility.

Other Things to Beware of

For every birthmother there will be different events that will trigger memories and dredge up the pain all over again. Some of these events include seeing babies on television, in commercials, in magazines and in malls. Seeing a child may trigger questions. Are they the same age as your child, and then it will hit you: someone else is pushing your child through a mall.

You may receive reminders of your birth experience if you live at the address you gave the hospital. You will begin to get mail for new mothers and babies. Be prepared for this and ask someone to intercept the mail so you won't have to see them at all. You can't and shouldn't live in a vacuum, but you can be aware of those things that trigger waves of emotions. You shouldn't avoid such things, you just need to be aware of them. Know too that while you will never, nor should you, get over this experience, time and distance will help diminish the pain.

Chapter 11 — To Do List

Birthparents

- Talk
- Allow yourself to grieve
- Admit your perspective on life has changed and learn who you are now.
- Some of your friends won't understand
- Try and find people who do understand and support you and your decision
- Reach out and stay involved in life
- Be aware of unexpected reminders and waves of emotion

Support Network

- Listen
- Acknowledge and share the grief
- Help focus on goals and the future
- Praise her courage, sacrifice, and love
- Try not to be affected by others' opinions
- Find someone to counsel and love your child

12

Moving On

Ruth's Story — A Mother's Heart

After the release of a child you grieve. It is truly like a death. For months your world has revolved around your child and the decision to parent or to release and now it is behind you. How do you move on? How do you pick up the pieces? Slowly. I took great comfort in the Scriptures.

I found Isaiah 51:3 (NIV) that says, "I will look with compassion on all her ruins." Imagine God's look of compassion; the love, the tenderness and the gentleness as he surveys the ruins of the wasted landscape. Ruins usually mean failure, plans gone wrong, just bits and pieces scattered around. Our lives and hearts were in bits and pieces. As I looked back over the last months, all I could see were bits and pieces. But his look does not condemn or blame. He sees hope where others see failure. He binds up the broken. He specializes in restoration and builds a future — and it is a good future. He puts the bits and pieces back together again to build his dwelling place.

What happens next? Well, Windsor and I remembered and talked about the memories with each other. We looked at pictures. We knew we would never forget and that we would survive. The heart mends slowly, and usually not in a straight line. Some days I thought it was over and I had moved on only to have the grief triggered when I least expected it. Once I was scheduled to speak at a ladies' luncheon in the city where Windsor's baby's adoptive grandmother lives. It did not cross my mind that she might attend the luncheon until I was getting dressed the morning of the event. My stomach tightened and tears filled my eyes. My emotions caught me off guard.

Moments like this occur; they are normal in the process of recovering from grief. I had to give myself grace. It takes time and could not be rushed. Each recovers in unique ways. Windsor was often upset with me because I did not show my grief in the same way she did. She needed me to cry with her; I carried my grief inside. To be honest, the pain was just too great to share with anyone but God. There are those who say sorrow is halved when shared. Perhaps. Grief is messy and I needed to have some sense of order in my life. One way I deal with pain and loss is to get busy, get my mind off of it. That isn't always good and it doesn't always work. Windsor read my behavior as uncaring. For months I had tried to take care of Windsor. I had taken the brunt of her anger and pain. Now, although I did not neglect Windsor, I had to deal with this sorrow in a way that enabled me to survive and move on.

And I remember. Each Christmas I send a gift to the charity of my choice — some charity that cares for children — in the little girl's name. I find comfort that she will know that each year her birth-grandmother remembers her. This is not intrusive in the life of this little girl or her new family and it gives me a way to remember.

In moving on I kept reminding myself that failure does not have to be final. I had hope in God's ability to restore. I have found that to live fully is to live in double reality, to know my pain and doubt, but also to know God's love. He has not forgotten or abandoned me. He doesn't let me just muddle through the best way I can — he is with me. He will strengthen me and guide me — if I let him. Most of the time I struggle to do it on my own. The Scriptures tell me over and over again that he will give me the strength I need. He is with me in the midst of my heartache. He knows all about what I am feeling — he has walked that same road.

He knows what life is like. Jesus not only experienced life here on earth in all it's agony, but became what I am, human, so that he could understand fully and comfort me in my need. He knows what it is to be an outcast, to be rejected, humiliated. He knows physical and emotional pain and mental anguish. He has wept over his children, too. He knows what it is to grieve. And in him I found — and continue to find — the comfort and strength I need.

When all the questions are asked; all the answers demanded; after all the pain and loss; after all the self doubt, guilt, hurt, anger; when I have exhausted myself in the asking, arguing and demanding; I quiet myself and remember what King David said in Psalm 131:1: "I do not concern myself with great matters or things too difficult for me. But I have I have stilled and quieted my soul like a weaned child rests against his mother. Hope in the Lord from this time forth and for ever more."

And that is what I did and do. I find hope in the fact that God is at work in my life, the life of my daughter and grandchildren.

"My soul belongs to God I know
I made that bargain long ago.
He gave me hope when hope was gone.
He gave me strength to journey on."
— Jean Val Jean in Les Miserable

Sara's Guidance

Part of the grieving involves processing the event and experience, evaluating the details and facing the future. You don't want to move on and you don't want anyone else to move on either. You'd prefer to wallow in your hurt and anger and you don't want anyone to stop you. With your emotions emerging erratically, you don't believe you have any reason to even get out of bed, let alone get dressed and leave the house. Remember the tender moments you had with your child and allow yourself to grieve. Perhaps you're stuck on the idea that you are damaged goods, and no man on earth will ever look at you, let alone want to marry you. Might as well just pack up and go to the convent now. Again, this is a good place to remind you, and your parents, of the importance of counseling. Talking with a counselor or a support group will help you rebuild your self-image. It is not only okay to grieve, it is necessary. You cannot and should not allow anyone to tell you to get over it and move on. You will never completely get over it, you will, however, begin to move on. In time you will look back and honestly know you did the best thing for you and your child

To heal, set some goals for yourself. Go to college, finish high school, get a job: whatever you decide, planning for the future will help you to heal faster and see that your experience was not in vain. Make your child proud of you; if you don't feel like moving on for yourself, do it for your child. Cherie, whom we have heard from previously, made the decision to release her son for adoption because she wanted to continue her education, go to college and have a career. She has done that. This past year her son celebrated his 6th birthday. Cherie currently works for a major insurance company.

Starting a new journal at this time, for life after birth, will also be extremely helpful. It gives you the chance to put those feelings, emotions and thoughts about your "new" life into perspective. Talking to friends, counseling and a support are also an important part of this grieving/healing process. Some people will listen for a while and then they may tend to pull away. It isn't that they don't care, they just can't do anything and they are frustrated with their inability to help in this situation. As well as writing, some women want to have something of a permanent nature as a visible reminder of their child. We would recommend planting a tree, shrub or bed of flowers that will bloom every year.

Cherie's Story...

Moving on is hard to do, but as you get more involved, time will pass and if you go day by day you will be surprised by how much time has passed. For the first year I remember every month on the 21st. I would think today he is 3 months old or today he is 6 months old and then think of how, in some ways, it seemed like just yesterday that I was at the hospital having that baby, yet in other ways it seemed so long ago that I held him in my arms.

I was planning on meeting with my son's father every year on his birthday for dinner, but that has yet to happen. I was never one to want to have my own big party for the baby to celebrate his birth. Every year around his birthday I get a little emotional and people call and e-mail me just to say, "Hey we remember and we think you made a great decision and did a brave thing. So it's nice, I know people care, and yes, they still remember.

I also have fewer pictures up now than I did years ago. Its not that I want to forget — How can I? But for me it's easier not to walk by the same picture of him everyday and think about it. I like to think of him and pray for him when he comes to mind. You may decide not to tell everybody about your child, especially as you get older and farther away from the actual adoption. Some people just don't need to know and as I said before some may even judge you and not take the time to understand. It's not like when you start a new job you want to run right in on your first day and tell everyone about your experience. When people ask if you have kids, I answer that question differently, depending on who is asking. I find it's just easier not to get into it and bring up feelings that go along with it. If a person stays in my life and I feel they need to know then I will tell them when I feel that time is right.

You will never, ever forget that child you carried beneath your heart for nine months and no one is asking you to, but moving on will help you and your child when you hopefully meet sometime down the road. You need to focus on your goals and ambitions and the more you do this the faster you will begin to heal.

Windsor's Story...

Today, I am a birthmother of a seven-year-old girl. I will always carry my daughter's newborn picture in my wallet. That is how I remember her. Today, seven years after I released my daughter to the Nelson's, I have learned to live without her. I will always have a hole in my heart and ache to hold my daughter again, that will never go away, but I have learned to live with it. I am blessed to see my daughter grow up in pictures and letters and know that she is being raised in the way I would have wanted.

You have made one of the most difficult decisions of your life, you've thought through a lot of issues and you've learned new things about yourself. You have found out you are much stronger than you thought you were, and you have found out the meaning of unconditional love. You will never forget your child, or the lessons you have learned. You have been able to handle things you didn't know existed before and you have matured beyond your years. Take all of this and use it to make yourself, your family and your child proud of you.

Postscript to Windsor's Story

As Windsor's Mom I want to tell "the rest of the story".

Windsor has productively moved on with her life. That is not to say it has been smooth sailing. Hardly. She struggles with her own regrets, choosing to forgive herself and others and, letting go of the anger. It is a process to which she is committed. Each day she takes another step forward, some days it's three steps forward and two back. But the progress is measurable.

One summer, she learned of a fifteen-year-old who was pregnant living in Michigan. This girl's parents were divorced and her father had arranged for an abortion. Through the grapevine this girl had already heard about and contacted Sara. When Windsor heard of this, she asked Sara if anything could be done to help this girl. She wanted to do something.

Arrangements were made for this girl to live with Windsor and Walker. Windsor, with Sara's help, guided her through the pregnancy, the decision process, the choosing of the adoptive parents, labor and delivery. All of this brought up old emotions for Windsor but she was determined to walk with this young girl who had been forsaken by her family.

Windsor stood by her the night the baby was released to the adoptive couple. It was a night of chaos as the girl's father lost control of himself and acted out in an exceedingly immature way. Sara was comforting the young girl. Windsor saw how difficult the father's behavior was making everything as he broke promises and, made rash, impulsive new ones. He became part of the problem — if not THE problem. Windsor knew what the girl was going through and that she did not need to deal with the inappropriate behavior of the father. Her protective instincts rose up. Windsor took the father out of the room determined to get him out of the picture. As she was driving him back to the place he was staying, he became hysterical and Windsor had to put him out of her car. This was at about 2:00 AM!

My phone rang at about 2:15. Windsor was crying. She was not sure she had done the right thing. She was overcome by the renewal of her own emotions and feeling empathy for the young girl. I listened and reassured her. Windsor had placed herself in a difficult place but was determined to stand by and help the girl. I applauded her maturity and grace to handle that situation. I am not sure I could have done nearly as well.

At the end of the conversation she thanked me for all the love and support I had given her during her pregnancies. She appreciated it all so much more as she saw the selfish and immature behavior of other parents.

The young woman continued to live with Windsor until she felt she was able to go back home, which she eventually did.

I was so proud of what Windsor had done for that young woman. She was turning her mistakes into something of purpose. I know God has a special plan for Windsor for the future. God doesn't waste anything when we turn it over to him.

Windsor will graduate from the local community college and have her Real Estate license. She is a wonderful housekeeper and Walker is very well behaved, a true little gentleman. I take my hat off to her. She has handled a lot in her young life and I admire her strength, courage and determination.

We have grown closer in these years and become friends. It is a joy for me to see Windsor's maturity and the beauty develop.

For those of you who have daughters or sons dealing with an unplanned pregnancy, I want you to know there is hope. No matter how bad a situation may seem, it can be redeemed. We have all seen the picture of the old tree stump that looks dead but as we look closer we can see a tiny, tender shoot emerging — the promise of renewed life. So it is with our daughters and sons. Don't lose hope.

Chapter 12 — To Do List

Birthparents

- Continue counseling
- Pursue your goals
- Make a living memorial
- Allow your hurt and anger to come out in good ways, it is ok
- Don't let others tell you how you should feel
- Talk and remember
- Continue journaling
- Keep a scrapbook of your adoptive parents photos, letters, and updates
- Make your child proud of you
- Forgive yourself

Support Network

- Listen
- Remember
- Talk
- Support your child's goals
- Be proud of her decision and express it in many ways
- Weave this experience into the fabric of the rest of your life
- Live in forgiveness for yourselves, your child, and the birthfather
- Don't berate yourself

13

How Should The Church Respond To Unwed Mothers?

Tim Troyer

"What do they want to talk about with us?" That question had been churning around and around in my mind all evening as I waited for our guests to arrive at our home. Earlier that day I had received an unusual phone call from one of our church elders asking if he could bring his family to our house to talk with my wife and me. "Of course," I replied, but something in his voice kept me from asking "why?"

I was a bit nervous as I opened the door, but not as nervous as my guests were. As Ben, Bonnie and their four children sat down in our living room, I could see that some of them had been crying. After a few seconds of intense silence, Ben dropped the bombshell, "Pastor Tim, Melonie is pregnant. She is going to have a baby."

Instantly a barrage of thoughts raced through my mind: What shall I say? How do I respond? How can I give hope to this lovely 19-year-old girl while at the same time making sure that sin is dealt with properly, and provide comfort to the hurting family, as well as deal with my own newly triggered flood of emotions. What will happen to the baby? How will the church react to the news? "Lord, please help me!" And He did!

I have forgotten many of the events and crises I have encountered in the course of my ministry, but I will never forget that evening. I told our friends, "We have one opportunity to handle this situation right. Let's commit ourselves to doing it that way!" Ministering the Lord's grace and forgiveness through our empathy, sincerity, and loving attitudes for their dilemma, my wife and I assured them that we would stand with them and help them as a family through this tough time. Over the next few weeks and months, I learned lessons about people having real experiences with a real Jesus! I don't assume naively that I handled the crisis perfectly, but walking this young girl, and he family through repentance, forgiveness and restoration taught me lessons about God Himself, myself and those in need. Here are a few of those lessons:

1. **Focus on people, not on problems.** It is too easy for people's problems to eclipse the fact that they are people who need God's help and mercy. It is often tempting for a pastor to do damage control and to try managing the problems of the people instead of identifying with them as persons and the issues they face. Frankly, that was my temptation at first with Melonie. Part of me just wanted the

problem to go away. I was tempted to make decisions and manage the information of what happened based on what I thought would keep the fallout to a minimum, protecting the reputation of our church, myself and others.

That was the wrong attitude! My heart is deeply moved as I remember that Christ was called "a friend of sinners." I am inspired and challenged by His constant willingness to bear the sins of others and to become of "no reputation" in order to redeem us. He doesn't just want our problems to go away. He wants us to know that He loves us completely and will never forsake us — even when we bring shame to His great name.

My wife and I made a deliberate decision to stand with Melonie and her family privately and publicly. We told her: "We will go through this with you," and then we made every effort to live out that important commitment. Unfortunately, the young man, who was the father of the baby would not take responsibility for his actions. His father was on the pastoral staff of a church in our area, and he and his family chose to distance themselves from the "problem". It was very tough.

I have seen many examples of people who were wounded by the Body of Christ at a time of their greatest need and vulnerability. Sad to say, the Church is not always a safe place in which to confess sin and to receive forgiveness. This must change! When we refuse to identify with people who are troubled or suffering and to restore then to fellowship through love and humility, we create the illusion that image is more important than anything else. Many Christians cluck their tongues and shake their heads over the sin of abortion. However, we can unknowingly create an emotional environment where a young girl out of wedlock would rather commit that sin than to face being mistreated, ostracized and humiliated by fellow Christians.

I have counseled with young ladies in my office, who have wept as they told stories of receiving pressure from Christian parents or relatives to have an abortion who, above all else, wanted to protect their reputation and that of the Church. That is the worst kind of hypocrisy and very damaging to the whole body of Christ. In our wish to keep sin exceedingly sinful and not compromise our beliefs, we must also be careful not to victimize the very people Christ died to save and to minister to.

It is amazing how one can know the Scriptures without really knowing or understanding the heart of God. The Pharisees devoted themselves to studying, memorizing and applying the Scriptures to every minute detail of their carefully scripted lives. But they didn't know the heart of God! All that is God's heart stood there before them in the person of Jesus Christ, and yet they could not see God! Jesus told them "You diligently study Scriptures because you think that by them you possess eternal life. These are the Scriptures that testify about me. Yet you refuse to come to me to have life."(John 5:39,40)

Consider the case of the woman caught in adultery and brought to Jesus. These men knew that adultery was wrong but did not know that God's heart was to forgive repentance and to cleanse this woman caught in the act. They wanted to kill her and appealed to obedience to the law as their mandate. It is sad too, that the man who was also caught in the act was strangely not accused and absent from the attempted stoning. Why the double standard? Why is this often the case even today? Usually the person who has to bear the public shame and emotional stoning is not the young man, but the woman who finds herself pregnant out of wedlock. The Bible indeed is the sharp sword that it declares itself to be. But when wielded without understanding the heart of God who forged the Word, it can hack to pieces the very people it was meant to protect, rescue and to heal.

Jesus, the Living Word said: "Let him who is without sin cast the first stone!" But no one dared to do it. The only man in the accusing crowd without sin was Jesus. He could have cast the first stone and allowed this woman to be stoned by the crowd. But He didn't. The man with every right to accuse, with every right to condemn, with every right to kill — spoke Life! He said "Women, where are your accusers? Has no one ever condemned you? Neither do I. Go now and leave your life of sin!" (John 8:9-11)

2. **Deal Openly and Tactfully, as you are able.** I do not believe in airing people's dirty laundry in public. However, when sin is known publicly, dealing with it in an open and tactful way can be powerful and redemptive. Melonie knew

that it was impossible to hide her pregnancy, because in a short while nature would make this obvious to everyone who saw her. I counseled her and her family to deal with it just as openly. I suggested that Melonie immediately communicate with the rest of her family and tell them what had happened, confessing her sin to the people who were most important to her and letting them know about her repentance. I encouraged her not to say, "I made a mistake," or "This was an accident," but to say, "I sinned when I made the wrong choice."

Melonie bravely did that. She asked for forgiveness and prayer, and it was tremendously healing. It enables friends and family members to talk with her openly about her pregnancy and the struggles she was facing. The Bible speaks to the principle that he who conceals his sin will be ashamed, but he who confesses his sin and renounces it will in the end be honored.

After Melonie had the opportunity to tell her relatives and close friends, we had a meeting with the church leadership team. She talked with our pastors, our elders and their wives. We encouraged them to ask her any questions they had on their minds and to share any concerns for her which they may have had. It was a sacred meeting. Our elders and their wives told Melonie that they forgave her and would pray for her and for the child forming in the womb. She also met with our former pastor, who had retired, and his wife, and talked and prayed with them. Most of our leadership team found out about her sin and of her repentance at the same time, which was very helpful.

I advised Melonie and her family to talk with our congregation openly about this as well. That was scary for everyone. I didn't insist that this happen but left the decision in Melonie's hands. After praying and talking with her family about it, she felt that she should say something publicly. Our pastoral staff also prayed about it and decided that we should do this on a Sunday morning during our regular service time. We encouraged Melonie to invite all of her family members and friends with whom she had shared the information, and our church was packed! In addition, it happened that we had an unusually large number of visitors present, too. I was nervous and prayed, "Oh God, please help us today. I don't want us just to *seem* like a loving church. I want us to be one! Lord I don't want us just to *seem* to be a forgiving church. I want us to really be one! Help!"

After the song service, I prepared our congregation for Melonie to share with them. I did not tell the people what she was going to speak about. I mentioned that she had spoken with our leadership team about struggles in her walk with the Lord, and that she also wanted to speak openly about it to our church family. Our pastoral staff and her family stood with her on the platform as she read a brief statement to the congregation. Her words were well chosen and to the point without overstating it. She asked the people to forgive her and to pray for her.

I then stepped to the podium beside her and explained to the people that this was a teaching moment for all of us. I explained how serious it was not handling such a situation God's way, but emphasized the rewards and blessings of forgiveness and God's mercy if done in the right, loving manner. It provided a perfect opportunity for me to talk about being a redemptive community and creating a safe environment in which to confess our sins to each other and to pray for one another too. I concluded by saying that the Lord had forgiven Melonie and we as pastors and elders had forgiven her too. All that was left now was for the congregation to forgive her.

Then, acknowledging the visitors to the audience, I addressed them as well. "You are representatives of the larger body of Christ. Will you also forgive Melonie?" Then I asked for all who sincerely wanted to respond to her request for forgiveness, as they felt led, to stand to their feet. People began standing, with many of them crying. And then spontaneously they began pouring to the front of the sanctuary to hug Melonie and her family. It was one of the most powerful worship services in which I have ever participated. After singing a concluding hymn, we prayed a prayer of remittance and commitment to the Lord. We then dismissed the service.

The outpouring of love and support was amazing. Visitors from out of town shook my hand at the door and told me that they had never been in a service like that before. Melonie got cards and letters from all over the

United States from people who had heard what had happened. The most important result of all this to me was that Melonie felt forgiven and could smile and hold up her head in our church. She would be facing some tough consequences from her decisions, but one of those would not be shame or disassociation from our church family.

There are no Illegitimate Children. None of us chose our parents, and none of us chose the circumstances surrounding our birth. In His tender love, the Savior bore the stigma of illegitimacy. He was accused by many of having been conceived out of wedlock and was even mocked by the Pharisees about it. I am touched in my heart to think that He bore it all with such dignity and without defensiveness. I am amazed that God chose for His Son to enter the world into the arms of a young, unmarried girl who would even be misunderstood by Joseph, her betrothed.

3. **There are no illegitimate children.** There are only illegitimate actions. Each human being conceived is deeply loved by God the Father and has a special intended place in His kingdom. Melonie and her parents wrestled with the option of giving the baby up for adoption or keeping the child. I encouraged them to pray carefully about this knowing that God loved this child more than any of them did, and that He had a plan for the child's life. I told them of one of my cousins who had been adopted and what an important person he had been in my life. Melonie and her family decided to keep the baby, feeling that in this situation

it was God's will for them. I knew this before she spoke with our congregation and was able to tell them that I was looking forward to the day when we would be dedicating her child in our church before the Lord.

When the time came for Melonie to deliver the baby, it happened to be on a Wednesday evening. I had to laugh at the timing of it. Most of our people were in small group Bible studies all over the community. Everyone heard that Melonie was giving birth to the baby and were all praying for her. After Bible study, I went to the hospital and found that the child had already been born. She was a beautiful, healthy baby girl. Announcing it in church on Sunday, we prayed for Melonie and the new baby. I think more people visited the hospital to see Melonie and her baby than any other child ever born in our congregation. It was amazing!

We deliberately chose to recognize and celebrate this child and Melonie as the mother. We dedicated her to the Lord several months later on a Sunday morning and again spoke tactfully and openly about the whole situation. On Mothers' Day, along with all of the other mothers, we gave Melonie a flower in order to recognize her too as a mother. We did not single her out or make any comments publicly. We just told her privately to stand with all the other mothers when they stood to be honored. My wife and I made it a point to talk with her that morning and to tell her how proud we were of her, and that we thought she was being a good mom. I told her that I am committed to pastoring her daughter, and that we would always be there when she needed us and would help in any way we could.

Melonie struggled. She went through some hard times and bore some tough consequences. But it also drew her closer to the Lord. It was during that time that she began really to seek God when she woke up at night to feed her hungry baby. It was also during those times when she became serious about her walk with the Lord and made a commitment to purity and to seeking His will for her life. She became an inspiration and encouragement to younger people in our congregation. Her faith and commitment to Christ became solid as she studied His Word and committed to doing things in His way. She did experience some painful treatment in the community and hurtful gossip. Thankfully, it wasn't from the hands of any people in the church.

The birth took place eleven years ago. What has happened to Melonie since? She met and fell in love with a fine, Christian young man, and they got married. I had the great pleasure of conducting the wedding ceremony. What happened to the baby? Melonie's husband adopted her child, and she has grown up calling him "Dad." I have the wonderful privilege of being the eleven-year old child's pastor. She is a very special girl and is loved dearly by her family, grandparents, church members, and classmates. I have a dream. If the Lord tarries for another ten or fifteen years, I want to see her walking down the aisle of our church, dressed in white, at her own wedding. I want to conduct that service to...and witness God's faithfulness to a new generation.

14

Summary On Adoption Law

Debra Fox, Esq.

Overview

Because the laws of adoption vary from state to state, there is no uniform adoption law throughout the entire country. Yet, there are common threads that link the laws of every state. What follows is an explanation of adoption law, without regard to any particular state's law. This is meant to be an introduction to people involved in the process of adoption. However, for guidance as to the laws of a particular state, please contact an experienced adoption attorney in that state.

Agency vs. Private Adoption

When a woman first discovers she is pregnant, and considers the possibility of adoption, she may ask what legal steps do I need to take? One issue that comes up immediately is the need for counseling by a caring professional. Usually this is a service that can be provided to a birth mother free of charge. There are two types of adoptions available in most states: agency adoptions and private or independent adoptions. An agency adoption means that the birth mother contacts a licensed adoption agency to assist her in finding a family to place her baby for adoption. The advantages to agency adoption are that they are licensed by the state, and therefore monitored on an annual basis for compliance with appropriate laws. For example, most states do not allow a person to work at a licensed adoption agency who has been convicted of a crime or accused of child abuse. Also, the state visits the agency once a year to review existing files to insure the agency is complying with all laws. Agencies are allowed to provide counseling services to birth parents and adoptive families. Counseling is important because it helps a birth parent thoroughly consider all of her options besides adoption, such as foster care, parenting, or having a family member parent the child.

A private or independent adoption is one where no agency is involved, but instead a private adoption attorney handles the case. In some states it is illegal for an adoptive family to reimburse a birth parent for counseling expenses in the context of a private adoption. If no agency is involved to provide that service, the birth parent may not be able to afford counseling, and may not receive it. This is a disadvantage to private adoption in some states. On the other hand, some birth parents prefer working with an attorney over an agency for personal reasons. It is always important in a private adoption to understand who the attorney represents. In most states it is illegal for one attorney to represent both the birth parents and the adoptive family, due to the inherent conflict of interest. Usually the adoptive family hires an attorney, and the birth parents have a separate attorney. Sometimes it is legal in certain states for the adoptive parents to reimburse the birth parents for legal expenses. Some birth parents choose not to hire their own attorney at all. Some states do not require that birth parents be represented, if they choose not to be.

Facilitators

Operating apart from licensed adoption agencies and attorneys are facilitators. These people usually ask adoptive parents to pay them a fee to assist them in identifying a birth mother who will place her child for adoption with them. The fee is usually used for widespread advertising, such as in yellow page books. However, in many if not all states, facilitators cannot do more than match a birth mother with an adoptive family. That is because if they do, they will appear to be operating as an adoption agency without a license. Licensing is required before somebody can operate an adoption agency. Because facilitators are not licensed, there is no supervision or quality control by the state.

Legal Documents

Once a birth parent decides whether to work with any agency or private attorney, there is the question of what legal papers need to be signed. Most if not all states require that a birth mother wait until after she delivers her baby to sign a consent or surrender of her baby for adoption. That is because it is one thing to consider adoption while pregnant, and it is another to follow through with that decision once the baby is in the world. Some states have no waiting period after the baby is born, and allow the birth mother to sign a consent immediately. Others require that the birth mother wait anywhere from 24 hours to 10 days before she can sign a consent. The thinking is that after a woman delivers a baby, she goes through emotional and physical changes that could interfere with her ability to make a good clear life decision. The issue of signing a consent is one which can differ between birth mothers and birth fathers.

While nearly every state requires that birth mothers wait until after they deliver before they can sign a consent, many states now allow birth fathers to sign any time before the delivery, after the birth mother learns she is pregnant. The rationale behind this is that sometimes birth fathers who are in the picture earlier in the pregnancy and therefore available to sign a consent, may not be easily found after the birth of the baby. If a birth father is willing to consent to an adoption, most states feel it is important to give him that opportunity even before the birth of the baby. After all, birth fathers do not go through much of the same physical changes that birth mothers do after birth.

Revocation of Consent

After the consent is signed, some states allow the birth parents to revoke it, or change their mind about the adoption. In other words, if a birth parent decides he or she made the wrong decision in placing the baby for adoption, there is sometimes a window of opportunity to regain custody of the child. The laws vary very widely on this subject. For example in some states, once a birth parent signs a consent at 72 hours after the birth of a baby, it is considered irrevocable, meaning the birth parents' rights are forever terminated. In other states, the signing of a consent does not terminate parental rights. Instead, it is viewed as showing the birth parents' intent to place the child, but their parental rights may not be terminated until a hearing takes place months down the road. In that intervening time between the signing of the consent, and the termination hearing, the birth parents would have the right to change their mind.

In every adoption there comes a point when a birth parent can no longer change their mind. Sometimes it is upon the signing of the consent. Sometimes it is once a Judge signs an order terminating the parental rights of the birth parent after a hearing. And sometimes it doesn't happen until the signing of the final adoption decree by the Judge. But once one of these events occurs, States feel that there should be some finality and security for the child, making it impossible for a birth parent to defeat an adoption.

Minor Birth Parents

If a birth parent is considered a minor, some states have extra requirements about who must be notified. The definition of a minor varies from state to state as well. It can be anywhere from 16 to 21. However, the most common definition of a minor is somebody who is younger than 18 years of age. Many states require that if a birth parent is a minor, the birth parents' parents must be notified of a hearing that would terminate the parental rights of the minor. Some states go one step further than mere notice to a birth parents' parents: they require that the parents of a minor also consent to the adoption. More progressive states, however, no longer require the consent of minor's parents. It makes good sense for a birth parent to notify his or her parents of their intention to place a baby for adoption as soon as possible, since the Court will usually require this anyway. If a minor's parents disagree with their child's wish to place their baby for adoption, many courts will weigh the maturity and competency of the minor birth parent against the minor's parents reasons for not allowing the adoption

One scenario where a court might go against the wishes of a minor birth parent to place a child for adoption is if the minor parent's parent is raising a sibling of the baby. Many courts do not wish to separate siblings if it can be helped.

Birth Fathers

Many birth mothers wonder whether they have to inform a birth father of their pregnancy and their desire to place a baby for adoption. Regardless of what state a birth mother lives in, she is required to identify a birth father if she knows who he is. That is because birth fathers, by virtue of being biologically connected to the child, have rights to the baby, just as the birth mother does. Even if the birth mother only knew the birth father for one day, and he never supported her during the pregnancy, or asked after her, he still has the right to know that he is the father of a baby, and oppose an adoption if he desires. Even birth fathers who are serving time in prison have rights to their children. Do not assume just because a birth father has had little contact with a birth mother, or he is not living a model life, that his rights will automatically be terminated.

Many times a birth mother will state that she knows the first and last name of a birth father, but not his current whereabouts. In those instances, a diligent attempt must be made to find the birth father and notify him of the adoption. Many states have paternity registries which provide a birth father with an opportunity to notify the state that he wishes to claim paternity to a child he knows will be born or has been born. In some states, if a birth father fails to register, he cannot be heard to assert any rights to a baby.

Even if a birth father does not sign a consent, in most states, his parental rights can still be terminated. So long as he is not opposed to the adoption, he is not required to sign any documents in order for the adoption to move forward. Many birth fathers do not realize that allowing their child to be placed for adoption relieves them of any child support obligations forever. That is because an adoption severs all rights a biological father has to his child. He is considered a legal stranger to his child once his parental rights are terminated. By the same token, he would not have the right to visit with the child, unless of course the adoptive family entered into an open adoption agreement with him.

When a birth mother is married to a man who is not the biological father of the baby, he is often considered the "legal" father of the baby. Many states presume that if a baby is conceived while the birth mother is married, her husband must be the father. Therefore, those states that make that presumption require that the husband consent to the adoption. If he chooses not to consent, then his rights need to be terminated against his will, or on an involuntary basis. Some birth mothers do not want their husbands to know about the adoption, perhaps because they have been separated from them for years, and do not wish for them to know their personal business. Unless such a birth mother can produce a divorce decree, long separation does not relieve the need to notify the legal father of the adoption. Perhaps one way of not telling the legal father is if the biological mother and father are willing to submit to DNA testing, proving they are in fact the baby's parents, and thereby ruling out the legal father as the actual father. Whether or not this can be done depends on the willingness of the Judge in the state before whom a birth parent will appear.

Reimbursement of birth parent expenses

The issue of whether or not a birth parent can be reimbursed for living expenses related to the pregnancy, birth and delivery of the baby, also varies from state to state. Some states have very strict laws disallowing reimbursement of any expenses except for medical expenses of the baby or birth mother during the pregnancy and delivery. Other states allow the adoptive family to reimburse a birth mother for such expenses as housing, food, maternity clothes, counseling, and transportation. Those states that allow adoptive parents to reimburse birth parents for these expenses usually require judicial approval. On the one hand it is argued that reimbursement of these expenses can look like bribery or coercion. (If you let me adopt your baby, I'll give you money to make your life easier). On the other hand, many birth mothers face extreme financial hardship in deciding to continue an unwanted pregnancy. Some birth mothers cannot continue working and may have no way of obtaining clean, safe housing during the pregnancy if not for the help of an adoptive family.

Open adoption

In most states, it is possible for an adoption to be "open." What this means is that there is some level of contact between the birth family and the adoptive family. This contact can be anything from having an intermediary send letters and pictures back and forth, while maintaining anonymity between the parties, to visiting one another periodically in one another's homes, and knowing one another's names, and addresses. Usually, in order for identifying information to be revealed about a birth parent or adoptive parent, the party whose information will be revealed has to consent to the release of the information. One of the most common types of open adoption is one where the adoptive family agrees to send letters and pictures through their agency or attorney to the birth parents several times per year.

Most states do not have provisions in their laws for what happens if an adoptive family fails to live up to their agreement to maintain some sort of open relationship with the birth parents. A dissatisfied birth parent could bring some kind of legal action against the adoptive family, but there is no guarantee that they would prevail. Most states look at adoption as the severing of one set of relationships (the birth parents to the child) and the establishment of another set of relationships (the adoptive parents to the child). However, in at least one state, there is a provision in the law for the birth parents to have recourse if an adoptive family fails to live up to their end of the bargain. However the law states that even if there is a legal dispute on the issue of openness, it cannot interfere with the finality of the adoption itself.

Conclusion

When each state draws up its adoption laws it seeks to balance the rights of all of the parties to the adoption. The different parties to an adoption consist of the birth mother, the birth father, the adoptive parents, the child, and the grandparents of the child. Many times the wishes of all of these parties do not coincide. When that happens it is up to a Judge to decide. Usually the guiding principle is what is in the best interest of the child. Some states give more weight to the rights of birth parents, such as when there is a longer period of revocation (or when a birth parent can change their mind about the adoption). Other states attempt to give finality to an adoption sooner, terminating the birth parents' rights early on in the adoption process. States also vary on how easy or difficult they make it for a birth father to assert his parental rights if he objects to an adoption. Grandparents have varying degrees of rights, depending on what state is involved. Finally, living expenses are allowed in some states and denied in others. This article attempts to highlight the issues which may arise in any state, without specific reference to any particular state.

15

What Do Adoptive Parents Go Through?

Susan and Matt Hancock

After going through two very different adoptions, we can safely say that, as a general rule, anyone who goes down the path of adoption should really be sure they want children. The road to "finalization" is filled with every emotion and anxiety that you can handle. In fact, without God we would not have been able to see our adoptions to completion.

The paragraphs that follow provide a brief overview of some of the memories and feeling that we experienced in our adoptions. It would be fair to say that our second adoption tested our metal at every turn, and the majority of the more dramatic feelings discussed below were not as present in our first adoption.

In both cases the involvement, or lack thereof, by the birth mother and birth father had a direct relationship on the security and emotions that we felt. Generally the more they were involved prior to the birth the more vividly we experienced the emotions outlined below. Of course every birth mother and birth father are unique and their attitudes and personality greatly affect the relationship and feelings experienced by the adoptive parents.

Here are some of the feelings that we experience on our journey with adoption:

Infertility

When we decided to adopt we had already traveled down the infertility path. This path for both of us was invasive, mechanical, and invaded our privacy. Certainly it seemed hopeless — trying anything to have a child with continued failure. We learned how to be patient and deal with the repeated hopes of pregnancy only to have them dashed when we did not get pregnant each month.

This process takes years and is expensive and time consuming. It is easy to blame the other for the problem, or to really get down on yourselves. We tried to continually focus on the plan that God had for our family — whatever that might be?

Adoption Preparation

This is probably the most frustrating parts of the adoption process. Once we had finally given up hope on having our own child, we then considered adoption. But by this time years had gone by! We were so ready to start the adoption process it was hard to have to complete all the paperwork. Caseworkers asked very intimate and embarrassing questions. Writing autobiographies, trying to distill the essence of our family history into a couple of pages for a "profile", which acts as your "adoption resume" where we were essentially trying to sell ourselves to a potential birthmother.

There were also background checks, reference letters from friends, and then a Home Study. There is a tremendous amount of scrutiny and work, and it is expensive at every turn. If you do not have thousands of dollars at your disposal adoption may not be available; and if it is you may find that others are way ahead of you in line.

Initial Interest

After waiting what seems like an eternity, and watching all our friends have perfect babies we finally got **the** call — someone liked our resume and wanted to meet us! They also wanted to meet two or three other couples, but we were at least in the running. This is when you question everything about yourself. You wish you were better looking, had a better house, or had something more interesting in that resume!

Interview

The big day finally arrives; we get to meet the birth mother and perhaps the birth father if they are still a couple. It is easy to lose perspective and feel as if your whole focus for the past year boils down to this meeting. Forcefully, we remind ourselves that God has a perfect plan for our family and try not to get too uptight — it helps a little!

Now we meet with the birth mother — someone we have never met or even spoken to before this day. It helps that a third party is present, usually from the adoption agency or in our case she was a wonderful woman who had taken in and counseled the birthmother in her time of need. Regardless of who is present, we have to hope that she finds us acceptable in the hour or two we have to put on our best face. It is so difficult; we have so much riding on that moment!

Selection

Our prayers had been answered — she picked us to become the parents of her child! This is a feeling of euphoria probably like finding out that we are pregnant! We immediately called our entire family and all our friends to tell them the good news and the due date. At the same time we reminded them, and ourselves, that she could change her mind at any time.

Now we go into "the baby zone". With some lingering caution, everything we do and talk about until the birth revolves around the baby. Picking a name, decorating the nursery, boy or girl? For hours we discussed what the baby would look like, whose mother will come to stay first, and for how long. As with any baby, it is the biggest event in our lives and deserves all our attention. Suffice it to say that if the birth mother were to change her mind at this point we would be devastated! That thought keeps us up a night!

Waiting

Although we have much to keep us busy, it is hard to wait for the big day to arrive. We want to let the birthmother know we support her, but how close should we get to her? She may want a lot of contact, which may be okay, but that can also cause tremendous anxiety. We are afraid if we do not agree to all of her requests she may get upset with us and change her mind.

As the birthmother makes each request we find ourselves asking the question: what should we do? Will she change her mind if we don't let her see our house or spend the day with us? Are we worried that if she knows where we live she may change her mind after we have had the baby for a month or more? Would she ever come and take the baby?

This is where it is great to have the adoption agency or counselor provide some guidelines that everyone can live with. We have a comfort zone and the birthmother certainly needs to know the baby is going to be well cared for. Like all relationships — understanding and compromise are important.

The Handoff

Depending on the situation, actually receiving the baby can be the hardest part of the adoption process. If the baby is in foster care or being held by a state or local agency then the process may be relatively simple. In our second adoption the birth mother wanted to personally hand the baby to us. As you can imagine this was an unbelievably emotional event. Although the baby was only a few days old, the bond the birth mother felt was very strong. For our part, we felt as if we were almost stealing the baby away from her.

Of course the attitude of the birth mother is very important at this stage. In our case, is was the hardest thing she had ever done and was very evident in her tears and emotional outbursts. Even with prayer and no time constraints, the situation was almost too stressful to handle. In biblical terms — there was weeping and gnashing of teeth from the birth mother! If we adopt again, we would prefer an intermediary to deliver the baby to us.

Keeping In Touch

During the first few months the demands that a baby places on you are overwhelming — your time is gone and their time is all that you consider. Every decision is based on how it affects the baby. It is at this time that you start to feel like you are the real parents of this child. Without you this child would be helpless.

You have two conflicting emotions. The first deals with the fact that you are the primary caregivers and the second deals with the reality that without the birth mother you would not have this beautiful child. So, you know that it is important to keep in touch with both birth mother and birth father, but you also feel like you need some time to bond and start your own family

The emotional stability of the birth parents will once again dictate how smoothly this part of the process goes. Some may want more contact and pictures while others may want to forget or not dwell on the issue. Both of our adoptions would be characterized as "open", so we send pictures every 3-6 months depending on where birthdays and holidays fall. At times keeping in touch is an effort. Life is so busy with the kids, house, pets and work. On the other hand, we are so thankful for the birth parents that we don't ever consider it a burden.

Meeting with the birth parents is another matter altogether. In the first year, parents spend so much of their lives taking care of the kids that we do not want to even consider that anyone else has a claim on the child. Although we know that the birth parents will be involved in their lives at some point, it is scary to meet with the birth parents. We wonder if they will think she is as special as we do and want them back — especially after we have gone sleep deprived for the first year or two.

In reality the birth parents just want to stay in touch, but as the adoptive parents we are naturally protective of our little treasure.

In summary, without faith in God, I don't know how adoptive parents deal with the stress throughout the whole adoption process. For instance, when we were writing our profile, we could have totally stressed out about making it absolutely perfect. However, no matter how good ours was someone else might have a better one? With God, we did our best and prayed that God would cause our profile to strike a chord with the right birthmother. Throughout the entire process, which is fraught with worry and doubt we had faith that God was in control. He doesn't promise that everything will turn out the way we want it to, but he will help us through the tough times. Every person has different burdens to bear in life — when God makes it clear that you will build your family through adoption you need to be ready for some curves in the road.

16

The Story Of An Adopted Child

Eric Bungo

One of the preconceived ideas most people have about adoption is that those children who are adopted will have serious problems later in life, all of which can be traced to their being adopted. The young man I interviewed for this section of the book actually volunteered to have his story told.

Eric is a 24-year-old young man, the middle of three children. His older sister is also adopted and his younger brother is the biological child of his parents. Being adopted is something he says he has always known. His parents gave him a book about adoption when he was very young and the word and concept became a part of his life very naturally. He was 7-8 years old when he remembers actually understanding what adoption really meant, and it made him feel special. He said at school when his classmates found out, they acted as though they felt sorry for him. He never felt sorry for himself and he and his sister would make fun of their brother, teasing him because he *wasn't* adopted.

Eric did feel that his parents played favorites with his brother, but as an adult, looking back on his childhood, he sees that was not the case at all. He remembers his mother crying just as hard as she spanked him, as she did with his brother. He has always felt very loved by his parents, sister and brother. Interestingly, he said that he and his adopted sister have seldom talked about the fact that they are both adopted and their feelings surrounding that issue. He said they have a silent understanding that they know how the other thinks and feels.

When I asked him if he would consider adopting he emphatically said, "Yes!" He feels that every child should have a two-parent home and he would also consider releasing a child of his for adoption if he was not able to provide for it in that way. He really had very little that was negative to say about adoption, except he wished he knew more about his birthparents. He thought the idea of open adoption was really "cool" and he was somewhat envious. He has a natural interest in his birth parents, wanting to know if there are any medical conditions he should be aware of. As for feeling as though he missed anything, he is grateful to his parents and has nothing but good feelings for adoption.

Eric is one of many people with whom I have spoken regarding their adoption and while there will always be adopted children who do have problems, there will always be children who are not adopted that have the same problems.

About The Authors

Ruth Graham McIntyre

ruth@forpregnancyhelp.com

Born in 1950, Ruth is the third child of Evangelist Billy Graham. Ruth is a published author and national speaker. She received a degree in Religion/Communications from Mary Baldwin College and for 11 years served as acquisitions editor for Harper Collins San Francisco. For 5 years she was Donor Relations Coordinator for Samaritan's Purse International then took the position of Major Gifts Officer at Mary Baldwin College.

Because of her own teenage daughter's two pregnancies, she has a heart for young women who face the choices of an unplanned pregnancy. She is open about her experience with her daughter and talks honestly about their choices and struggles. She is an effective and experienced communicator. For the past three years, Ruth has traveled the country sharing her experience as a source of information and encouragement. Now collaborating with Sara Dormon, they have developed a resource of choices for unplanned pregnancies: forpregnancyhelp.com.

Ruth is the mother of 3 grown children and grandmother of two. She is married to Richard and lives in the Shenandoah Valley of Virginia.

Contact toll free: 888-800-4440

About The Authors

Sara R. Dormon, Ph.D.

sara@forpregnancyhelp.com

Sara Dormon is a clinical psychologist specializing in issues surrounding women and crisis pregnancies. For the past 25 years, she has worked with young women and their families as they faced an unplanned pregnancy and the choices this situation brings. Her own personal journey has given her this passion and desire to help these young women. She and her family have taken many young women into their home and she has counseled them through the process. Whether they choose adoption or parenting, she helps them plan and prepare for their choice.

She has been a board member and counselor at the Amnion Crisis Pregnancy Center in Bryn Mawr, PA and has done extensive post-abortion counseling. She has done television and radio interviews covering the issues of teen pregnancy, abortion and adoption. Until recently, she had a private practice in Lansdowne, Pennsylvania. Sara is an experienced and humorous speaker who brings a refreshing and honest look at some very difficult issues.

Sara is the mother of three sons and the grandmother to three girls. She lives in a suburb of Philadelphia with her husband Bill.

Contact toll free: 888-800-4440

Adoption Profile

Hi! We are Eric and Cheryl. We are a happily married Christian couple who are emotionally and financially ready to start a family. Since we have not been able to conceive a child of our own, we are turning to adoption to make our dreams of having a family come true.

We own a home in a small suburb of Atlanta, Georgia. Our neighborhood is full of children of all ages and we look forward to birthday parties, Sunday school activities, having friends over after school, family vacations and helping our child experience the joys of childhood.

Eric is an attorney for a mid-size law firm in Atlanta. He enjoys sports, playing guitar, teaching Sunday school, and coaching a local girl's soccer team. Cheryl is a special education teacher who finds working with middle school students with learning disabilities both challenging and rewarding. She also enjoys sports and gardening. Cheryl is ready for a career change and being a full-time homemaker and mother is the career that she hopes to pursue.

Deciding to place your child in an adoptive home takes a great deal of courage and a tremendous amount of love on your part. We admire and respect your decision because we know it was a conscious choice.

We hope you are looking for a home like ours for your baby.

Sincerely,
Eric and Cheryl

Other Resources

The Complete Adoption Handbook Kay Marshall Strom and Douglas R. Donnelly. Zondervan Publishing House, 1992, $8.99, paper, 224 pp., for counselees
> **Description** Authors Kay Marshall Strom and adoption attorney Douglas Donnelly guide readers through the considerations and legalities that surround adoption and on to the final question: Is adoption for you? Contains a series of outstanding appendixes that include legal details state-by-state, additional resources, and reading.

No Easy Choices *The Dilemma of Crisis Pregnancy*, Sylvia Boothe. New Hope, 1990, $3.95, paper, 76 pp., for counselees
> **Description** There are no easy choices for the young unwed mother. But there are ways to help her as she makes one of the most important decisions of her life. This book helps provide guidance and help for the concerned Christian who wants to minister to a woman with a crisis pregnancy. Whether you wish to be a part of an on-going ministry, or want to help one young woman, No Easy Choices can help you. Discusses single parenting, marriage, and adoption.

The ProLife Corporate and Legal Handbook Thomas Glessner. Care Net, $5.00, paper, a reference or academic work
> **Description** Up-to date information for all pro-life organizations. Includes details for incorporation, tax-exempt status, and legal liability. Also contains copies of necessary legal forms.

Help and Hope for Teenage Mothers, Our Times Video. Ave Maria Press, 1992, $24.95, video, 28 minutes, for counselees
> **Description** This video explores ways to help young mothers, focusing on such issues as health care, education, bonding between parent and child, surrogate families, peer support, and negotiating adult versus adolescent issues.

Pregnant and Single *Help for the Rough Choices*, Carolyn Owens and Linda Roggow Zondervan Publishing House, 1992, $7.95, paper, 144 pp., for Counselees

> **Description** A sensitively written book presenting practical advice for the single woman who finds herself pregnant outside of marriage. It is a handbook and a guide for those facing pregnancy.

The Search for a Past *The Adopted Adults Unique Process of Finding Identity*, Jayne Schooler. Pinion Press, 1995, $10.99, paper, 200 pp.

> **Description** Written for adults considering searching for their birth family. Will help prepare them emotionally and psychologically both for the search and what they'll find. Also an essential resource for adoptive parents, spouses of adoptees, adoption counselors and agencies, ministers, and care-group leaders.

How Could This Happen? *Dealing with Crisis Pregnancy*, Laurie Taylor. New Hope, 1992, $1.95, paper, 19 pp., for counselees

> **Description** This book is written so that teenagers can understand the difficult decisions that their friend must face in dealing with crisis pregnancy and how they can help. This booklet is part of the Between Friends series.

Should I Keep My Baby? *Warm, Practical Help Teenagers Facing Pregnancy Alone*, Martha Zimmerman, Bethany House Publishers, 1983, $4-99, paper, 112 pp, for counselees

> **Description** A book especially written to teenage who are facing a pregnancy alone. Readers receive advice and encouragement for dealing appropriately with a sense of guilt, new feelings, physical condition, boyfriend, coming baby, future. A short, convincing presentation concerning abortion will gently but firmly lead readers away from this option.

A Hope Deferred *A Couple's Guide to Coping with Infertility*, Jill Baughn, Multnomal Books (Questar), 1989, $7.99, paper, 182 pp., for counselees

> **Description** Whether an infertile couple eventually has a child or not, takes second place to the agony of waiting, to the pressure of coping with a daily grief that affects every area of a couple's life □ from career decisions, to the marriage

relationship, to faith in God's wisdom. How a couple faces this crisis can mean the difference between times of destruction and bitterness or times of emotional maturity and spiritual growth. A Christian couple's guide to coping positively with the wait

Miscarriage *A Quiet Grief,* Nelson Kraybill and Ellen Kraybill, Herald Press, 1990, $1.95, paper, 16 pp., for counselees
> **Description** The loss of a baby through miscarriage can leave a couple filled with doubt, anger and many questions. Nelson and Ellen Kraybill share the struggle they experienced in dealing with this pain.

Empty Arms *Support for Those Who Have Suffered Miscarriage or Stillbirth,* Pam W. Vredevelt, Multnomah Books (Questar), 1984, $7.99, paper, 126 pp., for both **counselors and counselees**
> **Description** This book is the outcome of Vredevelt's search for understanding and encouragement. With the empathy personal experience brings, she is able to gently offer comfort to the woman who has just experienced miscarriage or stillbirth and insight to her friends and family who want to help and encourage effectively.

A Season to Heal *Help and Hope for Those Working through Post-Abortion Stress,* Luci Freed and Penny Yvonne Salazar, Thomas Nelson Publishers, 1993, $9.99, paper, 192 pp., for both counselors and counselees
> **Description** Written by two therapists who help women through post abortion stress, this compassionate book assures readers that their pain is a valid, natural response to a very difficult time. As they name and grieve their losses, healing begins. Contains hands-on tests, inventories, and lists to help women assess the extent of their pain and pinpoint where healing needs to start. Then readers can find healing from the guilt, shame, anger, depression, and sadness that plague them.

Help for the Post Abortion Woman Teri Reisser and Paul Reisser, Care Net, $5.95 paper, for counselors
> **Description** Written for women who think they may be suffering in the wake of an abortion. Also for loving family and friends, or those who desire to understand, help, or counsel women with post abortion syndrome.

Teenage Mothers *Their Experience, Strength, and Hope*, Andrea
Beauchamp, Resource Publications, Inc., 1990, $8.95, paper, 77 pp., for
counselees

> **Description** A series of stories, poems, Scripture, and
> photographs that depicts the experiences of teenage pregnancy
> and motherhood. Affirms the value of making pro-life choices
> when faced with teenage pregnancy.

The Complete Book of Baby and Child Care *Revised and Updated*,
Grace H. Ketterman, Fleming H. Revell, 1982, $12.99, paper, 560 pp.,
for counselees

> **Description** Revised and updated. A comprehensive and
> specific discussion of every aspect of parenting from prenatal
> considerations to parenting through age 12 and beyond.